Surveillance

Surveillance

A Concept of the Art

EDDIE CRUZ

ISBN: 1542803373
ISBN 13: 9781542803373
Library of Congress Control Number: 2017901467
CreateSpace Independent Publishing Platform
North Charleston, South Carolina
Cover art and illustrations done by Scott Simpson

In memory of my grandparents Eduardo León Cruz and América Guzmán León and my uncle, Jesús Noel León (Peter)

Dedicated to my wife, Shirley; my daughters, Serena and Alexis; my granddaughter, Selah; my niece, Stephanie; and my son-in-law, Greg. You guys have given my life purpose. I love you all, and may the Lord order your steps.

Contents

Our greatest fear should not be of failure but of succeeding at things in life that don't really matter.

—Francis Chan

1

Introduction

THIS BOOK IS specifically focused on the concept of surveillance as it relates to the private sector. It is designed with the novice in mind but is also extremely beneficial to those who have been in the industry for any length of time. It will also help those contemplating whether they should engage in this type of work.

"Private investigation" encompasses a large array of opportunities that are not limited to just surveillance. For example, some aspects of private investigative work include insurance fraud, vehicle-accident investigations, corporate fraud, criminal and civil matters, process serving, taking statements from witnesses, and doing background checks. Of course, you wouldn't know this from the response I get when I tell people that I'm a private investigator. They almost always associate me with someone who only follows cheating spouses. Domestic issues, like following a cheating or suspicious spouse, are usually referred to as matrimonial cases, and yes I do some of these cases, but they are only a small fraction of the many types of surveillances I've been involved in.

From watching TV and the movies, one gets the idea that surveillance is always fun and exciting. The truth of the matter is that it can be exciting at times, but most of the time it's boring. In this book, I will reveal the reality of this business and how to succeed.

I'm a retired detective from the New York City Police Department, where I operated as an undercover in the narcotics division. Besides purchasing illegal drugs, I was also exposed to, and invented, all sorts of tradecraft necessary to succeed in this business, which included surveillance. As an undercover, I was often under surveillance myself, either by my field team for protection or by the drug dealers. This gave me a unique perspective on surveillance from a different angle as the one being surveilled.

I was once involved in a lengthy major drug operation in which players of this drug connection where standing outside with me, talking. They didn't know that I was wired with a communication transmitter as one of them began to brag about how smart he was and his ability to avoid detection. As he said this, I also chimed in agreement and smiled for the camera, as I was able to locate the surveillance vehicle that was watching us and recording our every word. Due to my unique circumstances as an undercover, I was eventually conducting surveillances myself for all kinds of operations. I've also worked in multiple agency operations and was even selected to assist the FBI task force and the DEA task force during a couple of their operations. As a result, I've had the privilege of working with some of the best. I have also trained and guided undercover officers as well as investigators entering the private sector. So I have a lot of experience, and I'm well qualified to speak on the matter.

At the end of my career, I retired from a major case narcotics team and immediately took the test to become a private investigator without having studied the manual that came along with the application. I thought, "Why bother? How hard can this be?"

Boy, was I wrong. I remember that after I completed the exam, I was standing at the elevator bank with another man who had also completed the exam. I believe he was also retired from the police department. The two of us stood there just shaking our heads, and suddenly the other gentleman said, "You didn't study either?"

"Nope," I said. It was a funny and memorable introduction into the private sector. The exam had very little to do with police work but a lot to do with general business practices. In humility, I grabbed hold of the study material that had arrived with the original application and passed the exam several weeks later.

There is no doubt in my mind that surveillance in the private sector can and will be a humbling experience, especially for those of us who have retired from a law-enforcement agency. You no longer have the same authority or resources you once had, now that you are a civilian. You may have been an excellent police officer, but if you're not able to transform and tweak those skills, you're going to have a hard time.

The private sector is a whole new game filled with different challenges I will try to guide you through so that you will be a productive operator. Between law enforcement and the private sector, I have over thirty-two years of experience. With this experience, I will highlight and target the areas you will need to focus on if you want to succeed. I will define what surveillance is beyond a dictionary's description and demonstrate what it's really like in the private sector as opposed to what it's like in law enforcement. I will discuss the importance of preparing, planning, and strategizing before you go out into the field. This is a crucial step that is often ignored, unfortunately.

Next I will go over the two main kinds of surveillance, mobile (vehicular) surveillance and foot surveillance. Most surveillances are mobile, but every good surveillance operator is always prepared to engage in foot surveillance at any moment. This will be followed by the equipment that is essential in completing the job and bringing satisfaction to the client. This area is broad and fluid, as technology is constantly changing. It can also be very expensive.

After completing a surveillance assignment, a report of your activity and findings is usually required. There are perhaps many ways of doing a surveillance report, but I follow a timeline format. It's clear and to the point, and I will go into more detail in the Report Writing chapter, which will also include a sample report. Before concluding the book, I will add a personal note to prospective investigators (employees) and to the owners of private investigative companies. It's an honest and true assessment of my observations and experience in this field.

I have observed that many individuals who enter this field from law enforcement, including high-achieving units in their respective departments, have difficulty adapting to the dramatic change. Likewise, I've seen individuals from law enforcement with limited exposure to surveillance operations—even individuals with no law-enforcement background at all—excel in the surveillance component of private investigations. Either way, this should not discourage you because there are many other areas where one can still be an effective private investigator. For our discussion, this book will not delve into those other avenues because our topic here is strictly surveillance.

My goal here is to give you insight and advice regarding a unique field of work that also offers a manageable amount of flexibility with your time. I will share with you some of my experiences, ideas, and feelings concerning surveillance in order to best prepare you for what lies ahead. I strongly believe that I will provide you with a solid foundation that will assist you in pursuing this line of work and deciding whether this is for you.

Most of the things I mention in this book can be applied by all investigators and in many geographic settings, but let me inform you that I'm writing from the perspective of a private investigator who works on the East Coast in busy urban areas with multiple public-transportation systems, bridges, tunnels, taxis, airports, and so on. I also work in isolated suburbs that range from modest to affluent communities, and I'm aware of all the challenges that come with working in these settings. Having knowledge and proficiency on the subject of surveillance provides me a platform from which to give you an introduction into this unique profession. Let us begin.

2

Surveillance

THE GOAL OF every surveillance is to gather as much information about an individual or event without being detected. How you go about performing this operation effectively is the art. Surveillance, without question, is not easy and not just anyone is capable of doing it. It takes special individuals to be effective surveillance investigators or operators. That said, no one in this business is perfect. We all make mistakes, but these mistakes are great opportunities for us to learn and become better. With every mistake I've made, I've learned something new or at the very least confirmed something in my tactics that needed to change.

You cannot approach surveillance with a cookie-cutter mind-set because each surveillance is different. Add to that the idiosyncrasies of the subjects under surveillance, and you have an infinite amount of probabilities. With time, each successful investigator or operator finds his or her own comfort zone from which to operate—one that is balanced and not hindered by a predetermined outlook of the case. I say balanced because there is a healthy level of anticipation involved in surveillance. The anticipation I'm referring to is tied to your strategy, not the perception of how you think your case is going to turn out.

I incorporate the practical tools and strategies that I mention in this book, along with my instincts. From these things, I am able to anticipate what my subject (the person under surveillance) may do, such as the direction he or she may take on the way to work. This is appropriate and sometimes necessary, because unlike TV you cannot stand or park in front of someone's home and immediately engage them in a moving surveillance without becoming obvious. Your subject may even have a family member watching from a window, and your sudden suspicious behavior can alarm that person and cause him or her to alert the subject.

Properly anticipating the situation may even lead you to setting up an observation post (a strategically selected area from where you make your observations) around the corner. This method works for me more often than not, but it's risky and takes time and practice to develop.

One of the keys to surveillance is the early identification of your subject's behavioral patterns. Once this is established, you can anticipate properly without jumping to conclusions or severely miscalculating your subject. This leads me to other interesting observations I've made over the years, and that is the dichotomy between underestimating or overestimating a subject, or whether it's better to lose or be burned by the subject. "Burned" or "burn" is when an investigator or a location has been compromised and is no longer viable for surveillance purposes. Many surveillance operators struggle with these issues. Depending on the assignment, I may ask my employer beforehand if the target (another word for the subject or a location under observation) has been followed in the past, and if so, I'll make the necessary adjustments. If not, I typically lean more toward the side of underestimating them until they do something that makes me respect them, like a subject coming out of his or her residence and looking around left and right as if his or her head were on a swivel. This type of behavior will demand that I give them some respect.

Don't get me wrong when I say that I lean more toward the underestimating side. I'm not reckless, but if I apply all my tradecraft appropriately, I should be able to stick with the subject for a reasonable amount of time without being detected. Many operators overestimate their subjects, giving them way too much credit, and as a result they surrender too soon because the subject may have looked in his or her direction. On any given day, take notice of how many times someone looks in your direction when you're not even following that person. Or consider the lengthy distance you may have traveled alongside another particular vehicle that is not under surveillance. People naturally look around and travel in the same direction as you for extended periods of time. The key is to remain calm and to act normal when engaged in a surveillance.

The issue of whether it's better to lose a subject or risk being burned was something I initially struggled with. The problem was that I could not tolerate losing a subject. I wasn't getting burned for the most part, but I took too many risks because I was too concerned about losing the subject. I don't use GPS tracking devices because of all the legal ambiguities, so for me it's old-school surveillance. The conclusion that I've come to is that it's better to lose the subject than to be burned; if you lose the subject, you can pick up the surveillance again on another day or at secondary locations. But once you're burned, it's over. You can no longer go back on this target.

You've also ruined it for any other investigator to follow this subject because now the subject will be alert. Sometimes you may even have to deliberately release, or lose, a subject in order to preserve the surveillance. The subject may not be aware of your presence, but you've been tailing this individual for some time, following him or her down multiple streets without any buffer vehicles between the two of you to offer concealment. Your best bet in a situation like this is to get on a parallel street and attempt to follow in that manner. Otherwise, you will get burned. More on this later.

I've said a lot so far, but for someone to excel in this career, that person has to be dedicated to preparation, the cornerstone of every successful investigator or operator. Before stepping out to execute the operation of your assignment, you must always take time to prepare. This is paramount because it gives you the best opportunity to increase your chance of success every time. This doesn't mean you will always be successful, but on average, you will have a better outcome than if you don't prepare.

Operationally, you will encounter two main forms of surveillance: mobile (vehicular) surveillance and foot surveillance. However, on a rare occasion, you may come across something referred to as a "static" or "fixed" surveillance. In the latter, the investigator is not expected to exit the initial area of operation. The purpose of this investigator is to remain at the location to gather information and to inform possible team members located on the ground of the subject's direction of flight so they can initiate the moving surveillance when the subject exits the area.

The types of cases in the private sector that require surveillance are almost limitless. This variety helps to keep things interesting and provides a unique opportunity to observe human behavior at different levels of society.

Surveillance is demanding and requires a certain amount of stamina, patience, nerve, and creativity—not to mention the ability to remain focused in order to gather all the necessary information useful to your case. Skill is also important, but that takes time to develop. One can be taught the basics, but most of the progress is dependent on the individual investigator as he or she immerses him or herself into this line of work. If you're interested in this field and have no prior law-enforcement background, don't sell yourself short. Give it a shot; you just may have what it takes. However, if you come from a law-enforcement background, prepare to be humbled. I'll be the first to admit that it won't be as dangerous as police work, but this new game is no walk in the park.

On average, a surveillance can be anywhere from four to seventeen hours or more and continue for multiple days—or even longer. Occasionally, you are focused on a door, just waiting for your subject to emerge or arrive. I conduct many of these surveillances alone, but even if you have another investigator working with you, it's still a draining task. You cannot leave the location of operation because if you step away, when you return, you will not know if your subject has exited, arrived, or is still present at the location.

I understand that sometimes nature calls. For men, this may be a little easier to resolve—but not so with women. Each person has to consider how to resolve this issue on his or her own. It may be as simple as changing your diet either the day before or just before you go out or limiting your water or coffee intake (just not at the expense of your health). Hydration is important, especially in the summer. So don't take unnecessary risks with your health. Bring food or snacks so that you are not tempted to leave the car when you get hungry. Trust me, if you don't get hungry, you will probably need something to munch on in order to stay awake and focused on long surveillances.

In an ideal world, you would always have at least two investigators operating together during a surveillance. Two vehicles operating in tandem by two investigators provides a lot of flexibility as far as tactics are concerned and increases the chance of success in all settings while decreasing the chance of detection. In an urban environment, where there is usually a public-transportation system, you could have two investigators in one vehicle—one to operate the vehicle and the other to provide foot surveillance when needed, especially if the subject boards a train or bus. The only obstacle to having two or more investigators is cost. Clients usually don't want to pay for more than one investigator. I understand this can be an expensive investment, but the truth of the matter is that they usually end up paying more by using one investigator. Why?

If the investigator is working alone, he or she will have increased exposure to the subject, which calls for increased caution so as to avoid detection. This can lead to losing a subject prematurely and having to go back multiple times, whereas two investigators may have produced better results sooner. Although I'm a licensed private investigator, I've chosen to operate as an independent contractor, so I don't deal directly with the client. My employers do. But make no mistake about it—you will at times feel the pressure from the client as it trickles down to you. Clients can express their concerns and provide useful information, but they should not be allowed to direct the operation of a surveillance.

Good private-investigation companies are often under tremendous pressure to build a solid reputation and produce for their clients, which often includes a client who wants you to discover what he or she thinks or wants instead of the facts. This has always been one of my primary pet peeves about this business.

Listen, you should always want to do a good job out there for yourself, your employer, and the client. But this should not be at the expense of lowering your standards by manipulating or embellishing the facts. You have to embrace the fact that your integrity counts, whether others agree or not. If you're fortunate enough to work for a good company, this should not be an issue, but it's out there, and I want to make you aware of it.

Now, the issue of cost will not go away. It will always be a concern that will affect the number of investigators assigned to a surveillance. And even though I've finally seen a slight uptick in this area, expect to continue going out there on your own, which isn't such a bad thing in terms of your development. By going out alone, you quickly learn how to improvise and develop your skills in the art of surveillance because there is no one else to lean on. Being alone teaches you to remain focused, juggle tasks, and think outside the box. The outcome depends solely on you.

I believe it also helps you to get over that paranoid feeling that you have been detected, when in fact you haven't. This paranoia that you will be or have been detected is a common obstacle for many involved in this specialty of private investigations. I believe it's prevalent throughout the industry. It causes many to disengage from a surveillance far too soon, when in many cases, the subject wasn't even aware he or she was being followed. In my observations, this hesitation to engage a subject has often occurred at the start of a surveillance—that is, the minute the subject becomes active. This is one of the most critical points of the surveillance because it's when you identify the subject and begin to discern logistical patterns that will assist you throughout the remainder of your surveillance. If you've used proper tactics, there's almost no reason for your subject to become aware of you so early in the game. I have witnessed on numerous occasions investigators who disengage from a surveillance because of this concern.

And another thing I've observed is that this anxiety can be contagious. This happened during a surveillance I was involved in that required multiple investigators in multiple vehicles. An operator in this surveillance claimed that the subject looked in his or her direction, and within minutes, some of the other operators became spooked and began claiming the same thing. This caused a division in the team, and as a result, only a couple of us remained engaged. In the end, it turned out to be nothing, and the surveillance continued for several hours and days without any further issues. I hope I'm not sounding insensitive or proud here; I'm only illustrating a condition that I've witnessed too often in this industry.

When I first entered the private sector and began doing surveillances, I thought that it was easy and that anyone could do it. I never gave myself much credit for the work I did. But after some time working in various situations with many different investigators, I've come to understand how difficult this work truly is for just anyone to do it. So I'm not minimizing the difficulties and challenges that present themselves in this line of service. I completely get it: only those who do this work can share that feeling that comes over you when a subject looks in your direction. But working in a team all the time doesn't really help you to overcome this anxiety when it's not warranted. What ends up happening is that those more skittish investigators tend to stand back and allow other investigators to do all the work, and that's not fair.

Working independently helps you fight through that because it's all on you, and there is no one else to share the blame if you fail. It exposes your abilities and deficiencies. Through this exercise, as you fight through your anxiety, you will soon realize that your subjects don't always know you're following them, and your confidence will begin to grow. However, just to be clear here, you are going to lose subjects in this business, and you are going to get burned. It just comes with the territory. And there are legitimate reasons for those things to occur. But sometimes it's due to poor tactics or giving subjects way too much credit in their ability to detect you.

We're going to go over preparation in the next chapter in greater detail, but to be brief, if you go over the assignment material that should have been provided to you at the start of your case and ask the right questions, your operation should go well without any need to hesitate once the subject becomes active. There are situations in which a subject has been followed in the past by another company—and in some cases even the client—and he or she has been detected. This is not a favorable situation for the next surveillance operator because the subject is now on high alert, but it can still be done if planned correctly. If you're in this business for any length of time, you're going to face scenarios like this. And there will be times when you will lose a subject because of unpreventable circumstances like a traffic condition. This will happen, and when it does, relax. If you've done your due diligence, that's all anyone can ask for. As far as traffic conditions are concerned, no one should be demanding you disobey traffic laws to maintain your surveillance. Your life and the lives of others are far more important than losing a subject.

And when you get burned, so be it. It happens. As long as it's not due to recklessness or poor work ethic, don't feel too bad. I've seen investigators go out there and get burned a lot when starting out, and that doesn't really get me upset if they're trying. After all, not getting burned isn't always a true indicator of skill. Sometimes the surveillance operator is just not making an effort, and *that* upsets me. In law enforcement, you can conduct a surveillance with almost unlimited resources and equipment, which aids tremendously in avoiding detection. But in the private sector, you're a one-man team. You're the surveillance operator, the cameraman, the note taker, the footman when called for, the operator of the vehicle, and so on, with no one else to relieve you. So it's tough work, even for law enforcement and all its resources.

I often recall an episode during my time on the police force. I was part of a team that was conducting a narcotics operation. It was a citywide surveillance involving several vehicles, and I observed a team member get burned. The subject walked right up to him in his vehicle and told him that he knew the officer was following him. I watched the whole thing unfold from my position and felt terrible for my team member. Up to that point, I had never had anything like that happen to me, and that moment was seared into my mind. I made a conscious effort to never allow that to happen to me.

Remember what I said in the introduction about this work humbling you? Years later, I retired and entered the private sector, and I recalled that day when one of my subjects approached me directly and stated the very same thing: "I know you're following me." I felt crushed that this had happened to me. It had been one of those last-minute surveillances that tend to come up every once in a while, when a client is giving you just one day to come up with the goods. So I went out there determined not to lose this individual, and it cost me.

Sometimes the pressure of a case overrides your good judgment and causes you to use poor tactics. It's not an excuse for me getting burned; that was on me, and I own that. But there's a fine balance in how I do a surveillance. I'm not going to tell you how to do yours. I'm only being transparent here to give you some insight into how I operate. I never ever want to get burned, but for the sake of a case, I'll take a risk every once in a while on the last day of operations when I haven't found what I believe to be a key element of the truth. But you have to be wise here. If you're doing a potentially hazardous surveillance involving drugs, organized crime, or a gang-related case—yes, you do get some of these in the private sector—you need to use proper logistical planning and common sense concerning your own safety.

There will be times when you notice a subject begin to become more aware of his or her surroundings. At this point, without panicking, you need to properly evaluate the situation and consider if there is sufficient reason to reel it in a bit to give your subject some additional space. If after your assessment, you've decided to loosen the reins on the subject and as a result lose sight of the subject or conclude that you must terminate the operation for justifiable reasons, then that course of action is acceptable; at this stage of the surveillance, you're trying to preserve it. You want to avoid any confrontation, and you don't want to further complicate things for yourself or others who may continue the surveillance after you, or in addition to you.

The ability to discern whether your concerns are valid will understandably take some time when you first start out in this business. While I advise that you push through your fear, I also strongly suggest that you use caution. An effective surveillance operator must find a tactical balance between being both aggressive and cautious at the same time. Too much of either will not benefit you at all. And no matter what stage you're in in your development, remember the phrase "space or terminate" when your gut starts telling you that something isn't right.

As this overview of surveillance continues, a clearer picture should begin to emerge on the uniqueness of this occupation. Work hours are generally nontraditional compared to the rest of society's, and you will find this provides a lot of flexibility that can be used to your advantage. As a surveillance investigator, you spend almost all of your time alone and in the field. The only reason for you to go in to the office is to hand over videos and photos or perhaps to pick up or drop off equipment if you don't have your own.

When conducting a surveillance, either alone or with another investigator, you're operating without any direct supervision. In the field, you're basically making all the decisions in relation to the assignment objective. You're not expected to be frequently calling your employer with every single detail that is occurring in your surveillance; a periodic update should suffice. Logical reasons to call in would be to obtain further instructions as it relates to the contract made with the client and to share important ongoing developments in the surveillance. Apart from that, there is a fair amount of responsibility placed on your shoulders, so you need to be a dependable and trustworthy individual. Due to the nature and fluidity of this profession, it is difficult to supervise investigators in the field, and the only way your employer can determine your integrity and performance is by your production.

Now, production doesn't necessarily mean that you must always provide evidence of the alleged act. In some cases the subject may not even materialize or be doing anything wrong. Yet production can be demonstrated by the notes you take of your actions and observations made while at the location of your assignment. Your notes and recordings should also reveal your time of arrival and departure. I've heard stories of investigators not even showing up for their assignment and claiming to have been there—or showing up only to fall asleep. Fortunately, this isn't a common occurrence. That being said, I think most in this industry will agree with me that good surveillance investigators are hard to come by. And those with good work ethic and integrity will at some point rise to the top and reap the rewards for their efforts as word spreads.

The one thing I love most about this work is that in the field, the street is your office, and I would encourage you to take every advantage that the street provides. To me, the street—especially in urban areas—is like a stage, filled with props limited only by my imagination. I'm dating myself here, but phone booths used to be a useful prop to use as an observation post back in the day. With the advent of the cell phone, you don't see many of those anymore, and being in one today would draw more attention to you. Nevertheless, there are still numerous things out there that can provide concealment. Street vendors, bus stops, restaurants, window-shopping—all provide you with opportunities to blend in.

Speaking of window-shopping, you can also use the reflection of a store window to monitor your subject as you pretend to be interested in some item. This is a common counter-surveillance technique, so be sure that your subject isn't using this technique on you as well. Office windows, car windshields, side-view mirrors from large vehicles, and even the reflection on the side of a clean vehicle can assist in identifying the location of your subject without you having direct eyes on that person. One thing to note here is that you never want to make eye contact with your subject. Use your peripheral vision to monitor.

To illustrate a real-life example in using the street, I recall a time when I was tasked with the responsibility of being a "ghost" for another undercover officer who was making a large narcotics transaction. "Ghosting" is when you blend into an environment, unnoted by anyone, to gather intelligence and provide protection to another officer. In this case, the transaction was in an urban, residential neighborhood with nothing to conceal my presence nor to provide me with an excuse to be there. As I looked around, I discovered an abandoned car tire and got an idea from my experience growing up in the city. I picked up the tire and began rolling it close to where the transaction was to take place, under the guise that I was attempting to sell the tire. I'm not sure if this sounds strange to you, but in the neighborhood I grew up in, selling car tires in this manner was a common form of survival for certain individuals.

Anyway, this action allowed me to speak to pedestrians and buy time—not to mention the fact that it made me look pathetic and non-threatening, which is exactly what I wanted. I've also used restaurants that provide an unobstructed line of sight to the subject or target location. However, suburban and affluent communities present the biggest challenges because they often lack commercial buildings, stores, restaurants, and other things that are available in the city. Foot surveillance in this type of setting is virtually impossible. When on a mobile surveillance in the suburbs, you have to be even more creative because sitting in your car for an extended period of time will at some point draw attention to you. You need to learn how to hide in plain sight.

One thing I've done in situations like this is to park right behind a utility vehicle, like a landscaping truck that may be doing work in the area or a construction site. This makes me look like I'm part of the action. I got this idea from observing the owners or managers of contracted companies as they pulled up to a location in a civilian vehicle to check on their workers. Landscapers don't care for the most part because they're busy working and are not concerned with your reason for being there. You can also park by a home that's for sale and appear to be interested in the property. Neither of these options is going to buy you a whole lot of time, but they will work temporarily until you have to resort to other measures.

The last resort would be to do what I call spot-checking. In spot-checking, you park totally out of sight of the target location and perform periodic drive-bys or foot surveillances to check on the status of the subject. Some areas require you to do this because it is impossible for you to be the only car parked on a block for any length of time without being detected. Imagine yourself coming home and seeing a strange vehicle parked in your neighborhood with someone sitting inside for a long time. You're going to get concerned and call a neighbor or the police. In some situations, the concerned neighbor may even call the subject you are watching.

Events like this happen to investigators all the time, so you need to implement legal yet unorthodox methods in order to avoid as many interruptions to your operation as possible. Once you acquire your subject's patterns and direction of flight, you can begin expanding the surveillance zone. I do this quite often and with a high degree of success after I've determined the likely direction of travel. On one occasion I set up an observation post half a mile away from the subject's residence. I parked my vehicle by a park and caught the subject's vehicle as it passed by each and every time for months without ever being detected.

This strategy may be a little uncomfortable, especially for your employer, but I can't think of another way to do this and still have success. The only issue with this strategy is the frequent drive-bys you have to do when conducting spot-checks, because essential to the art of surveillance is the ability to be "quiet". Quiet, for our discussion, means to be invisible and not noticeably moving around, and this applies to mobile surveillance as well as foot surveillance. I'll get more into this in chapters 4 and 5. So admittedly, spot-checking is not "quiet" because you're periodically driving by the target location, and with each pass you expose yourself more and more, not just to the subject but to neighbors as well. But you really have no other choice when it comes to situations you will face in suburban settings.

I've often told investigators cutting their teeth in this business that you have to discern when to put down the textbook on surveillance and adapt to the reality of surveillance in the private sector. Textbook surveillance works well in law enforcement because you operate within a team and have all the proper equipment, structure, and, arguably the best factor of all, time. Again, in the private sector, you're working alone more often than not, and the best equipment isn't always available. Add to that the fact that you're also working for clients who are usually operating within a budget and time constraints, and suddenly time becomes a limitation to your effectiveness. Many are the elements of a surveillance, and we're only getting started.

So far we've taken a bird's-eye view to set the stage for what really takes place behind the scenes and how a surveillance in the private investigative world should be conducted. But before we get into the meat of surveillance, we have to first set up a foundation that will guide you to success. And this foundation is the preparation and planning stage, the subject of our next discussion.

Key Points

- Understand that the key to surveillance is to be invisible.
- Accept that surveillance is not easy.
- Be balanced in how you conduct your surveillances.
- Focus on your subject's behavior patterns, especially in the initial stages.
- Overcome the fear that you have been detected when in fact you haven't.
- Remember that it's better to lose your subject than to be burned.
- Remain calm and don't panic when approached.
- Consider the appropriate foods when preparing for a surveillance.

- Stay hydrated.
- Avoid getting into accidents.
- Be "quiet" during your surveillance and limit your movements as much as possible.
- Use the street to your advantage and figure out ways to hide in plain sight.

3

Preparation, Planning, and Strategy

FOR THE SURVEILLANCE investigator, improvisation plays an important role in the course of a surveillance, but it should never be used as an excuse to neglect preparation and planning. Proper preparation also recognizes the need to adapt so you will not be caught totally off guard by the unexpected. The fact is that your subjects are not following a script. Preparation is a basic fundamental for every successful surveillance investigator. Legendary martial artist Bruce Lee said it best: "Advanced skills are the basics mastered."

From the moment you receive your assignment, your initial task should be to read all the provided information concerning your subject and familiarize yourself with this individual. In my situation, I'm usually e-mailed an assignment, which can include all or some of the following: case objective, subject's name, height, DOB, home address, place of employment, vehicle(s) assigned, secondary locations connected to the subject, and a photo if I'm lucky. You're going to find that clients who do provide a photo often issue one that is outdated, so you need to focus on your subject's features to see if you can detect a specific characteristic, or characteristics, that will help you identify the individual.

In examining the photo, you should focus on the following: eye color (although not always possible in a photo), eye shape, eyebrows, shape of the nose, shape of the lips, ears, shape of the chin, forehead, hair length, hair style and color, scars, tattoos, possible eyewear, and any jewelry or piercings. Identifying your subject from a photo is one of the hardest things to do in surveillance, even with a current photo. Clothing, especially sunglasses and hats, can alter someone's appearance and prevent you from making an early confirmation of the subject's identity. However, clothing can also be helpful in making an identification if what he or she is wearing in the photo is also what he or she is wearing on the day of your surveillance.

This is especially true when it comes to men and their footwear because they don't typically have a large selection of shoes. I remember using this method at an airport once. I had located a male that fit the description of a photo that had been provided to me along with my assignment. I wasn't 100 percent sure if this was the subject in question until I looked at his feet. That's when I realized he was wearing the same shoes that were displayed in the photo.

Once you complete your examination of the photo, I strongly recommend that you upload the photo to your phone. We'll go over technology/equipment in a later chapter, but if you don't have a smartphone, you should seriously consider one because it is an indispensable tool to have in this line of work. The reason I recommend that you transfer the photo to your phone is because printing a hard copy leaves you vulnerable to a momentary lapse when you may leave it on the seat of your car, visible for anyone to see, including the subject. The same is true if you're on a foot surveillance. You could accidentally drop the photo, and either the subject or someone who knows the subject could pick it up. So keep it in your phone, and look at it often until you commit it to memory. Also, be aware of your surroundings when looking at a photo. You don't want anyone to look over your shoulder and see what you're looking at.

Next on the agenda would be mapping out the location where the assignment is to commence before reporting to the location. If you forego this step, you place yourself at a disadvantage that robs you of the opportunity of preparing and strategizing for the unknown. Mapping a location is really an alternative option since most companies and clients do not authorize pre-surveillance, which is a physical reconnaissance of the area prior to the start of the actual surveillance. Fortunately, technology plays a tremendous role in surveillance operations, and now we can see the location for ourselves without even being present.

So how do you go about mapping out a location? You've probably figured this out already, but computers and smartphones make this simple. You can go to any map site such as Google Earth, input the location(s) of interest, and hit the "Map" and "Satellite" tabs to get different perspectives of the location(s). In either view, you should be able to get a pretty good idea of what type of neighborhood you will be operating in. Determining whether the area is commercial, industrial, residential, urban, suburban, or rural is vital to how you will prepare and what you can expect. It can also assist you in developing an excuse for being in that area should you be approached by a concerned citizen. In a residential area, for example, you can determine the type of housing that exists, such as whether there are one-family homes, multiple-family homes, or public housing.

As I mentioned in the previous chapter, one challenge I'm fairly acquainted with is conducting surveillances in suburban residential communities. Getting a satellite view of the location of interest allows me to see if there are vehicles parked on the street. You don't want to arrive at your assignment and be surprised to learn that your car will be the only one parked on the street, while everyone else is parked in driveways or garages. You have to plan for these situations, and knowledge beforehand can go a long way in finding a solution. Mapping out a location will also provide you with traffic patterns in the neighborhood and possible travel routes of the subject, especially if your assignment mentions the first location your subject is known to travel to. In some instances, you may even be able to see the target vehicle or street signs that reveal parking restrictions, such as alternate-side-of-the-street parking regulations. This advanced knowledge of the area of operation can assist you in picking an optimal observation post (OP), one that gives you good concealment or lessens the chance of being detected.

While I'm on the subject of observation posts, I would almost never recommend that you sit in front of the target location unless it's absolutely necessary or you're working with a team and your sole purpose is to be a spotter in a nondescript vehicle that will not be following the subject. By operating in the capacity just described, the investigator positioned in front of the location will alert other team members that the subject has exited his or her location and the direction of flight. This technique is sometimes necessary because of complications in identifying a subject. It may be a domain with an attached garage occupying multiple vehicles and a door leading directly into the home.

In this example, if other people are living at this location and access to the vehicle is hidden from the street, you would need to know right away who is in which vehicle when it exits. You don't want a caravan of vehicles already strategically positioned in their observation posts moving without confirmation that they have the right subject. But even then, it's a risky proposition better suited for those with a lot of experience.

Personally, I always try to sit as far away as I can. This way, if I do raise suspicion, it will be by someone a reasonable distance away from the subject. It's a given that you will raise some suspicion in this work, so you have to strategize for that. I set up an observation post as far away as I can but with a direct line of sight to the target location. If I raise suspicion and feel the need to move, I'll have the space to do so without disturbing the immediate target area. This strategy can also buy you time. Positioning yourself a good distance away from the target location allows you to creep up closer when on long surveillances, and sitting in one spot for hours will bring unwanted attention. This tactic helps to preserve the immediate area surrounding the target location and prevents you from being detected prematurely by the subject.

During one of my lengthy surveillances, I had a resident who was not part of the investigation aggressively approach my vehicle, yelling and demanding to know what I was doing. I attempted to put his mind at ease, but it was obvious this guy had lost his mind. I simply rolled up my window and called the police to see what they would have me do. They could hear the guy screaming outside my car and directed me to the precinct. This is why it's never good to sit too close to the location where your subject is located. This guy drew a lot of attention toward me, and we ended up at the local precinct to resolve the problem before my subject could become aware of my presence. This doesn't happen often, so don't get too concerned. Just know that residents can draw unwanted attention to you.

Another thing that can draw attention to you is your vehicle. If you have a vehicle that is expensive, has a unique color, or even has something as simple as a sticker on your window or bumper, you can easily be identified. In the story mentioned above, I had been following this subject for a lengthy period of time, perhaps months. At some point during that time, on an off day, someone had sideswiped the left front-end panel of my vehicle while it was parked. The car was operational, but I had a significant dent and knew I had to get it fixed soon, because I feared that otherwise it would make me noticeable during my surveillances. Well, the guy who had yelled at me mentioned he had known I was in the neighborhood before because of the dent in my vehicle. I have a common vehicle with a common color that allows me to blend anywhere; the problem was the dent.

After familiarizing yourself with the subject and all the points of interest, you should begin to assess what equipment is necessary to execute the surveillance. Some of the essential items are a camcorder, a covert camera, a notebook or voice recorder, and a GPS with all the pertinent addresses related to your case already programmed into your device. If you have more than this and can manage bringing more equipment, then by all means, do so. You never know when it may come in handy. I carry two camcorders with me at all times, just to be on the safe side.

Once you've decided on your equipment, you need to make sure that you fully charge all your devices, and test them to make sure they are operational. Don't wait to test them in the field because that is not the place you want to discover a device is malfunctioning. Dead batteries can cause another unforeseen problem that will ruin your day. Most clients expect your video recordings to have a feature called a date/time stamp on them because it is useful evidence, and if the battery on your device dies, it can automatically go to a default setting, giving you the wrong date and time on your recording device. This will probably drive your employers up the wall, and you can't blame them. So it would be wise to always check that your time stamp is accurate. Also, be aware of time changes in the spring and fall because you want to avoid making recordings with the wrong time.

The indispensable item I alluded to before is your cell phone, preferably a smartphone. Smartphones provide many services for a surveillance investigator, and they absolutely need to be fully charged before you step out. Since the cell phone is so important, you should always bring a charger, not only for your phone, but also for all your equipment in the event of a lengthy surveillance.

A good piece of equipment to invest in is something called a "power inverter." It can be plugged directly into your cigarette lighter and comes with outlets and USB ports to plug in all your devices when conducting a mobile surveillance.

Once all your equipment is fully charged and operating, you need to check the weather and pick out the correct clothing that corresponds with the surveillance you're conducting. Most of my surveillance attire is dark or neutral in color; this way I can blend in and avoid standing out. I appreciate when my subjects wear neon or bright colors because I can spot them from a secure distance and recover them quickly in a crowd. This is why investigators should avoid wearing these colors—to stay concealed.

If you're doing a mobile surveillance, you need to prepare your vehicle by first filling up the tank. You don't want to be following a subject and suddenly have to disengage because you're running out of fuel. Also, be sure to fill up the night or day before; all sorts of things pop up on the day of the surveillance that will delay your departure time and cause you to be late. Before leaving the gas station, check to see if you have enough change in your vehicle. Many locations have parking meters, and having change on hand allows you to legally park quickly in case you have to initiate a foot surveillance.

Here on the East Coast, an EZ Pass is a must-have, especially if you are doing mobile surveillance. Often you will follow subjects through tollbooths, and you don't want to be restricted to the cash lane while your subject breezes through the EZ Pass lane. And no matter what kind of surveillance you're doing, you should always have a fully funded and current Metro Card for quick access to the public-transportation system in the event you have to initiate a foot surveillance.

Next on the list is a very important, yet often neglected, item: your car windows. Clients don't want to see smudges or dirt on your windows when viewing your recording of events. It not only distorts the view but also looks unprofessional. If you live in an area like mine, this can be a real pain. I've cleaned my car windows at times right before I leave for a surveillance, only to drive through a highway-work zone or arrive at a location where landscapers are working. In both cases, debris is tossed back on my windows and dirties it again.

Inclement weather is another unavoidable issue. What you can do is pull over just before you arrive at the target location, make sure it's a safe distance away, and clean your windows there. Include your side-view mirrors too. To further maximize visibility during a mobile surveillance, remove all the passenger headrests in order to eliminate any visual obstructions that may interfere with your navigation.

Finally, get yourself some entertainment for your vehicle. I don't mean a book or magazine; that will take your eyes off the target. I'm suggesting CDs or audiobooks that will help you stay focused on those long days that you're just sitting in your car waiting for something to happen. I have SiriusXM radio in my vehicle, and it's been worth every penny so far. I also have certain podcasts that are interesting and instructional in many areas, including private investigations. Surveillance can be long and boring, so you need to try different things in order to stay awake. If you're in a public setting with a lot of distractions, you can even get out of your vehicle and enter a local establishment like a fast-food restaurant or a Laundromat that has windows facing the target area.

The following is a checklist I've included to assist you in your preparation.

Checklist

- ☐ Review all the information regarding your assignment.
- ☐ Map out the location.
- ☐ Select your equipment.
- ☐ Preprogram all the addresses connected with your surveillance into your GPS before you arrive at the location.
- ☐ Charge all of your equipment.
- ☐ Check that your equipment is operational and that the date/ time stamp is correct.
- ☐ Carry extra SD cards for your recording devices.
- ☐ Carry a fully funded and current Metro Card.
- ☐ Check the weather forecast.
- ☐ Dress appropriately.
- ☐ Fuel up your vehicle.
- ☐ Clean all the windows in your surveillance vehicle.
- ☐ Prepare your food for the day: protein bars, protein shakes, and so on.
- ☐ Develop an excuse for being in the area of operation.

Key Points

- • Read the complete assignment and familiarize yourself with the subject and his characteristics if a photo was provided.
- • Map out the location(s) of operation.

- Analyze subject's photo for key characteristics.
- Preprogram a stand-alone GPS with all locations in connection to your subject.
- Avoid confrontation.
- Charge all your equipment.
- If you're on a mobile surveillance, make sure your vehicle has a full tank of gas.
- Avoid having a hardcopy of the assignment details.
- Avoid setting up observation posts that are close to the target location.

4

Mobile Surveillance

MOST SURVEILLANCES ARE mobile, meaning that a vehicle is involved and necessary to surveil a subject who may be traveling by car. Even if your subject does not use a vehicle to move about, your surveillance vehicle still offers excellent concealment from which you can make your observations. For mobile surveillance, a good and reliable vehicle is necessary. The vehicle should not have any significant scratches, markings, or visible damage like a dent. Remove or avoid placing bumper stickers of any kind on your vehicle or any other ornament or vanity license plate that can identify you. You should also be in a common vehicle that blends well everywhere, not a flashy car or one that can associate you with law enforcement.

Also, avoid large SUVs unless you're in an area where the vehicle blends in and the assignment calls for it. Some investigators like using minivans because of all the comfort and room they provide and the ability to make observations and recordings from the rear compartment area. Small-to-midsize SUVs are nice because you get some of the comforts of a larger vehicle, and there are enough of them on the road to allow you to blend in.

One of the arguments in defense of SUVs and minivans is that they allow you to see above the smaller vehicles so you can maintain unobstructed visual sight of the target vehicle. It's a good argument, but personally I prefer smaller vehicles because you can hide better, find parking a lot easier, and use fuel more efficiently. They also provide excellent maneuverability when you need to make quick moves or navigate in traffic. The smaller SUVs and crossovers provide this agility as well, and my only hesitation is that since they are taller than low-riding vehicles (sedans), they are more visible. Nevertheless, I must admit that due to the many years of surveillance, my back has taken a beating. As a result, I'm now forced to consider purchasing a small SUV.

The next thing to seriously consider is the color of your vehicle. Neutral or earth tones like gray, slate, green, tan, or brown are good selections. In my opinion, the metallic colors are also nice because they tend to disguise their true colors depending on the lighting conditions. Avoid white, yellow, red, or any exotic color that will draw attention to you. Some investigators recommend avoiding black vehicles, perhaps because pairing that color with tinted windows makes the car stick out a little more.

You're going to notice that colors play an important role in this business as we move on to the interior of the vehicle. Preferably, your interior should also be dark; whether it's leather or cloth doesn't really matter. A dark interior conceals you significantly if you're wearing dark clothing, whereas a light interior serves as a contrast to you or anyone else sitting in the vehicle, making you more visible.

The next item is window tinting. Before you decide to tint the windows in your vehicle, you first need to find out what the law is in the state where you reside and work. I mention where you reside and work because you may do some—or a lot—of work outside the state in which you live. There are different opinions when it comes to tinting your vehicle for surveillance. Some may say that tinting your vehicle makes you more suspicious and threatening. Others say that you should only tint the back three windows to avoid suspicion. Tinting the back three windows of your vehicle would indicate to me that you like recording from the rear seating area. That means you're going to be constantly moving from the front to the rear of your vehicle. You may even need to exit your vehicle to do this.

Everyone has his or her own style in this line of work, and if this suits you, that's fine. There are times when sitting in the back of your vehicle is totally recommended, and I do this from time to time when I feel it's necessary. You can even purchase a tension curtain rod and black curtains to divide the front seating area from the back, giving you outstanding concealment. I invented a similar contraption for those special situations in which recording from the back was necessary, but I'm not going to totally outfit my car to strictly record from the rear seating area. It requires too much moving around, and with all your equipment, something is bound to get lost. Plus, if you have to get in and out of your car each time to do this, that's more exposure and attention that you draw to yourself. I prefer to tint all the windows in my car except for the windshield. Once again, check the laws in your state, but you may even be able to apply something called a "shade band," which allows you to tint a small portion of your windshield that can act as a sun protector.

In any event, because the interior of my car is black, I don't even need to use limo tint because my dark interior enhances the darkness in spite of the fact that I use a lighter tint on my windows. You can also use a combination of different levels of tint. For example, I use a lighter tint for my front windows than I do for the rear windows so that I can see a little better at night and also be in compliance with the law. In the end, it's your decision and should be determined by the laws of your state and by your style and comfort in how you conduct your surveillance.

Operational

Now, let's get into how to conduct a mobile surveillance. In your preparation, you should have also activated your GPS to see how long it would take you to arrive at the location of your assignment. You want to consider traffic conditions and roadwork at the time of your departure because you do not want to arrive late. Leave all your jewelry at home because rings, necklaces, and earrings shine and reveal your presence in the vehicle. Also, commit to memory at least one car plate that is related to your case; you may just bump into it as you near the location of operation in the event that your subject got an earlier start. All the locations in connection to your assignment should already be installed in your GPS so that you can have immediate access to them when called for. Later on, I'll explain how this can be even more beneficial.

Nevertheless, there will be times when your GPS will have difficulty locating specific addresses. In a number of such cases, I have found that my smartphone has saved the day through the map application—just another plug for why the smartphone is so essential for surveillance. Regardless of what kind of surveillance you are doing, it is common practice in the business to make a video documentation of your arrival at the area of operation (see sample report in chapter 7).

I've added a little twist to this by including my GPS in the video. Sometimes when I use my GPS to arrive at the location of my assignment, I record the GPS display on the forefront of my camera, while capturing the audio from the GPS stating that I'm arriving at my destination, as I record the target location in the background. This is not necessary and can be risky if someone is already outside. It's just something I throw in at times to show the time of my arrival and proof that I'm at the location. There are times when this may be called for but definitely not mandatory. I also try to quickly gather as much information as possible when I first come up on a location so that I don't have to keep going back. Continually going back to the target location to collect pieces of missed information only increases the chances that you will be detected.

One benefit of arriving early at your assignment provides you with sufficient time to set up and canvass the area for an ideal observation post. Mapping out the location online from your home or office doesn't always reveal this. I once had a case in which the subject lived in a very tight community with narrow roads. It was imperative to observe this individual exiting his home and his activity in the garage area. After canvassing the area, I discovered that between two homes on an adjacent block, I had a clear line of sight of the subject's residence, garage, and driveway. It was a perfect location that provided concealment and also allowed me to see in which direction the subject would travel upon exiting his home. This location would not have been visible from computer satellite software. During your canvass of the area of operation, you also have the option to look for higher ground, which occasionally provides an excellent and secure observation post.

Canvassing the area may also include your search for vehicles associated with your case. When searching for vehicles, don't focus only on the make and model of the vehicle; look for the plate number as well. I can't tell you how many times I've been given the wrong vehicle description, only to find the right vehicle because I was looking for the plate number as well. It's not out of the question that your subject may even arbitrarily transfer his plate to a different vehicle entirely. Other times, the plate number may also be off by one character, so you need to be able to decipher that.

It is also wise to check on parking-restriction signs because they provide information that can assist in your strategy. Let's say your subject is parked on the side of the street where his vehicle needs to be moved by a certain time. You now have a window of time during which your subject should emerge, and you will be totally prepared. Another thing to search for is whether there are surveillance cameras at the target location or other homes in the area. You can't do much regarding the other homes, but you must stay out of view of the target location's cameras.

Like everything else, selecting an observation post is very important because it can set the tone for the rest of your surveillance. As I mentioned earlier, try your best to sit far away from the target location but still within sight. Avoid sitting in an isolated area if possible; otherwise, you can be easily identified. Parking among other vehicles provides some concealment and makes you less obvious.

Another thing you can attempt to do is to park with your back to the location. In this scenario, you can monitor the target location through your rearview and side-view mirrors. Some investigators are not comfortable with this, and I understand that. Watching everything directly in front of you is far easier than looking through your mirrors. But by sitting with your back to the location, you will easily deflect all attention away from the target location behind you. Once you have selected an observation post, monitor all the activity in the neighborhood in the early stages of your surveillance. Getting aquatinted with the dynamics of the community and the residents' schedules can prove quite helpful in selecting future observation posts in that area, should your surveillance require you to return.

After you have settled in, make sure that none of your case material is visible. Keeping it in the sun visor isn't always secure because if you need to step out to investigate something, the pressure from the wind created when you shut the door can cause all of your documents to fall on your seat and make them visible. Put them in a bag or a folder in that space between your seat and the center console.

Now that you're in surveillance mode, you have to be "quiet." Don't drive by the house frequently unless you have to park a great distance away and are forced to conduct spot-checks. In fact, if you have a good observation post, you shouldn't have to drive past the location at all. Driving around and getting in and out of your car could alert others to your presence. While in "quiet" mode, turn off all the interior dome lights above your head. Nothing is more irritating during a surveillance than when your interior lights come on by accident. Also, be careful with how loud you listen to your music or other audio; it can probably be heard outside your vehicle if it's loud enough. Keep the volume low, and if your vehicle is equipped with Bluetooth, invest in a Bluetooth headset that will also alert you to incoming phone calls. Furthermore, be aware of your surroundings, especially when recording. Pedestrians tend to come out of nowhere when you least expect it and may walk up on you.

On that note, you should already have a plan in place in the event someone comes up to you and asks what you are doing. Whatever you do, don't tell them what type of case you're doing if you decide to tell them that you're an investigator. If you're doing an insurance case, tell them you're doing a matrimonial case instead. Some in the industry may disagree with revealing to someone that you are an investigator, but I do this often, and it tends to work. I'm a man, and I tend to make people nervous, so putting them at ease is a priority for me. Female investigators have a tremendous advantage here and are able dissuade the concerns of neighbors with much more success.

Without being too specific, in some neighborhoods it's a good idea to inform the police ahead of time that you will be conducting a surveillance in their precinct. This is strictly a courtesy, and significantly reduces tension with the police because some of them get upset when they have to respond to a suspicious vehicle in the neighborhood without knowledge of your presence. If they ask me what kind of case I'm doing, I'll tell them something completely opposite—just like I would for concerned neighbors—because you never know if they know the subject. And when you are approached by either a neighbor or the police, don't panic and take off. Even if you're confronted by the subject, remain calm, and use your excuse for being there. Suddenly taking off is a dead giveaway, and you can forget about ever returning.

Another thing you can do is get a fake work ID that you can hang on your rearview mirror or place on your dashboard. This gives the appearance that you're there on official business and temporarily calms nervous neighbors. I have a fake work ID that identifies me as a route inspector. I use this job title to inform people that I'm there to see if and when a certain package will arrive. So far, it's worked. The only thing is that you have to be careful not to use the name of a company already in existence—that's illegal. Just make up a name, and see if it exists. Once you've found an unused company name, you can go online and search for companies that create ID cards. If you're going to get one, make it look official by adding your photo and a barcode. Like everything else, make sure there aren't any legal concerns regarding you having a fake ID for this type of work.

Another thing I often do is lower the sun visors in my car to further limit any visibility inside my car. I also keep the visors down when driving, but you must be careful because they can also blind you to traffic lights and other traffic devices. If you're conducting nighttime surveillance, you need to be aware that your subject may see the light emitted from your car and devices. Therefore, you need to be careful—especially when recording with a camcorder—that you try to hide the light emitting from the LCD screen. You can purchase a hood to install over the LCD screen of your camcorder, and this will allow you to view what you're looking at and prevent the light from illuminating your face.

Finally, we're up to the part where you're waiting for your subject to emerge. Whether you're working by yourself or with another investigator, you need to be completely focused and observe everything surrounding the target area. Don't depend on your partner—if you have one—because your partner may be depending on you. We'll get into report writing later, but you need to document as much information as possible about the target location, including information about all vehicles that may be connected to the location. You can also use a voice recorder to take notes because it allows you to quickly document information without taking your eyes off the target. If you haven't done this already in the planning stage—and you have good information about the first location where the subject may go—now would be a good time to set that secondary location as a desired destination on your GPS to see the route the subject may take to get there from the starting location. This will allow you to anticipate what direction the subject will travel and how to proceed.

As you wait for your subject to emerge, you may need to turn your vehicle on to use either the air conditioning or heat, depending on the season you're in. However, because most vehicles nowadays have daytime running lights, you need to find out how to shut those lights off when sitting in your observation post. In my vehicle, if I pull up the emergency brake and then turn on the car, my headlights will not come on. You definitely need to figure this out for nighttime surveillance. While waiting for your subject to emerge, be aware that most vehicles today have alarms and remote car starters. These are great for an investigator; it's an early warning that your subject may be about to come out. As you're starting to see, a lot goes into conducting a surveillance before your subject ever emerges.

When your subject does finally emerge, fight that urge to quickly turn on your car, or the subject may hear you. As he pulls out of his driveway or parking space, try to delay as much as possible before initiating your moving surveillance. One determining factor is if there is a traffic light at the end of the block. In that case, you will have to move a little quicker. Also, be careful as you exit your observation post so that you do not pull into the road without checking to see if another car is coming. With all the adrenaline now pumping, it's easy to just pull out into the road without looking. In fact, if you're not in danger of losing the subject and you see another vehicle coming up the road, you can allow it to get in front of you to act as a buffer between you and the target vehicle.

Now that the surveillance has become active, you should attempt to acquire additional information about the vehicle that perhaps you were unable to obtain before. Search for stickers, rear-lighting characteristics or signatures, damage, and anything else that can aid in quickly identifying your vehicle in traffic. Many times, vehicles have stickers that indicate a club or a school that they or their children attend. This can be helpful in the event that you lose your subject in the vicinity of one of those areas because you now have a reference point you can canvass. If you're in an urban environment or a town with many vehicles on the road, it's OK to be directly behind your subject's vehicle for a reasonable amount of time, especially while you're traveling straight. When I say directly behind him or her, I mean absent of any buffer car between you and the subject's vehicle.

Avoid tailgating, and allow enough room for another vehicle to be able to slide in between the two of you. You can continue with this strategy while assessing your subject's behavior. Even if your subject is making multiple turns onto different side streets. By observing his or her body language in his or her vehicle, you can make the determination as to how close or how far to position yourself behind the subject. You can focus on your subject's rearview and side-view mirrors to see if he or she is frequently looking into them. If he or she is doing this frequently while traveling, it may be time to consider your options. But if he or she is on the phone or speaking to an occupant, this usually buys you a lot of time because the subject is distracted, and you can continue to remain directly behind him or her.

One other thing to consider here is the nature of your surveillance and if it requires multiple days of surveillance. If it's a surveillance that's going to carry on for several days or longer, you don't want to get burned or begin making the subject suspicious too soon. I like to gradually chip away and gather new pieces of information I did not have before, like what the subject looks like, places of interest, and directions of flight.

It's a process, and these little bits of information add up and assist you in your strategy and even in finding your subjects again when you lose them. I'm reminded of a scene in the movie *Zero Dark Thirty*. In it, the CIA is trying to locate a certain individual to confirm his identity. Once they zero in on a likely candidate, they take a quick photo of the possible subject and break off the surveillance. I love that scene because it illustrates my point. There was no need to jeopardize the case by continuing the surveillance, and a good piece of information was obtained. While active in a mobile surveillance, you can turn on your GPS and put it in map mode to get a picture of the area and where the subject may be heading. This is very useful because if the subject enters a dead-end street, you should be able to see this beforehand.

You do not want to follow someone into a dead-end street for two reasons: either your subject is on to you and is conducting a counter-surveillance move to identify you, or the subject is legitimately there, and following him or her into this area will significantly expose you, which may lead to you being burned soon afterward.

Another feature of the GPS that I use all the time is the Recent button, which displays all the recently added addresses. If there are multiple locations linked to your subject and you have preprogrammed all the locations into your GPS ahead of time, you should be able to see all the locations when you hit the Recent button. Next to the address of each location is the corresponding distance, which allows you to see the subject's proximity to each location of interest while a moving surveillance is in progress (see figure 1). This knowledge will assist you in anticipating the subject's moves and even activate your own directional/signal light before your subject does as you approach a turn that your subject is likely to make while traveling to a documented location.

In addition, I created my own app that may work even better than the GPS. It's a tool that investigators can employ to help them during a surveillance. I haven't published it yet because I'm still ironing out some issues. When and if I decide to publish the app, I will announce it on my website at Eddiecruz.net. Basically, the app allows you to see all the locations of interest at once on a map and your position in relation to each location in real time. You can also invite and share an ongoing case with another investigator who is working with you. When you do this, the two of you can see each other's locations, along with all the points of interest. Seeing all these locations on a map will give you an idea of what areas the subject frequents and is likely to visit. These locations can then be saved under a case title, date, and description for future use so you don't have to type the information all over again.

Figure 1

If in the course of your surveillance, you lose a subject, you can go directly to the closest area he may have been going to if it's within a reasonable distance. This also depends on how and where you lost the subject. If your subject made a last-minute turn in the opposite direction of the location he had appeared to be going to, you don't have to rush out of the area to get to that secondary location. Stay in the area or the exact location where the subject was lost. Many times the subject will return to that spot. Important to note here is that mobile surveillance does not exclude you from having to initiate a foot surveillance as well. Your subject may park his vehicle and enter a location of interest, and you need to further investigate where he or she may be going or whom he or she might be meeting with. You are not going to get this information by remaining in your vehicle unless the subject enters a location like a restaurant with large windows, thus allowing you to safely observe and record your subject from the security of your vehicle.

Now, suppose your subject parks his or her vehicle at a parking meter. I'm not sure about the rest of the country, but where I live and work, we have these things called Muni-Meters. You have to deposit a certain amount of money relative to the amount of time you're going to need your car to be parked at a specific location, and in return, you receive a small receipt. You are then required to place this receipt on the dashboard of your vehicle to inform the authorities that you are legally parked and for how long.

Well, this receipt provides some interesting information. It publicly displays how much time the subject is going to be away from his or her vehicle, which gives you a window of time before the subject returns.

I remember when I first got this idea. It was during that same surveillance I mentioned in chapter 2 that required numerous surveillance operators. It so happened that one of the investigators lost sight of the subject in a major commercial area. After canvassing the area, I located the subject's vehicle and noticed two things: it was unoccupied, and it was parked in an area with Muni-Meter parking machines. Now, finding the vehicle was great, but the objective of this case was to discover who the subject was meeting with. The idea of checking the Muni-Meter ticket came to me as I assessed the situation. Upon observing the receipt through the windshield, I was able to determine the amount of time we had to locate the subject. I initiated a foot surveillance and was able to locate the subject in a store.

Based on the time the subject needed to return to the vehicle, I positioned my team members at locations where we could intercept the subject. This is further evidence of the numerous benefits the street can provide.

Let's get back to mobile surveillance while it is in motion. The tactics used to surveil a vehicle on the road or in traffic vary when it comes to where the action is occurring. Surveillance in the city is different from surveillance on a highway or in a suburban neighborhood. In the city, where there are frequent traffic lights and numerous vehicles traveling in the same direction, one can—and should—maintain close visual contact with the subject, because one sudden turn at an intersection, and he or she is gone. The advantage of the city is that you blend well with all the vehicles, pedestrians, and distractions.

By the same token, these activities can also cause you to lose the subject. School buses, public-transportation buses, commercial vehicles, lost drivers, and pedestrians pose challenges to your success too. Nevertheless, the benefits far outweigh these challenges when you're conducting a surveillance in the city.

One that immediately comes to mind is how I have taken advantage of slow-moving traffic conditions. On many occasions, there has been an' individual of extreme interest inside a subject's vehicle whose identity is unknown. As traffic comes to a stop, I have carefully been able to capture and record the image of the person of interest by focusing my camera on one of the side-view mirrors. I do this because I never know if I am going to get another chance to identify this individual, and it also proves that this individual was in the subject's vehicle.

This technique works very well, but you have to be careful, even if you have another investigator working with you in your vehicle. As you move out of the heavily populated and trafficked areas and into the suburbs, you are going to need to change your tactics. You cannot follow a vehicle for a prolonged period of time without a buffer vehicle, especially when frequently turning onto different side streets along the route.

When you are in this type of situation in the residential streets of a suburb, there are a few things you can do. Number one is to maintain space, and whenever the opportunity presents itself, such as at a stop sign or traffic light, you can pretend you are going to park, but only if there are other vehicles parked on the same road. You can also pull into a parking lot if one is available and emerge once your subject is on the move again. Suddenly pulling over doesn't do much if there aren't other vehicles you can conceal yourself with. Provided that it's a two-way street and traffic conditions allow this, when your subject comes up to an intersection and makes a turn onto another street, bypass the intersection, as demonstrated in figure 2, make a U-turn, and reengage slowly.

Another thing I do when it looks like my subject is about to make a turn—and there is some sort of facility that allows me to drive across the parking lot and in the same direction my subject is heading—is to cut right through (see figure 3). If your subject is waiting at a light before he makes the turn, you can casually enter the parking lot and position yourself at the other end, ready to reengage at the appropriate time. Just make sure this is not considered a traffic violation where you live or work.

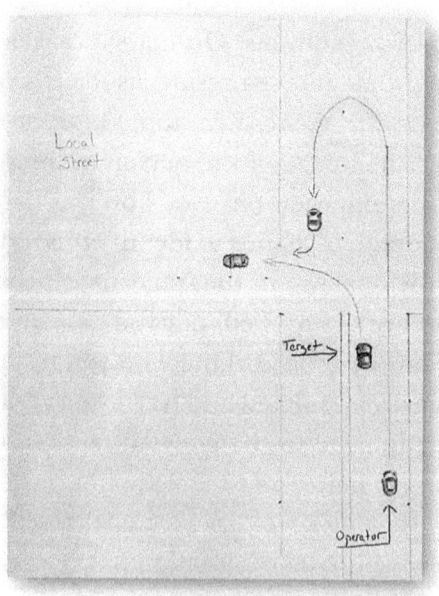

Figure 2

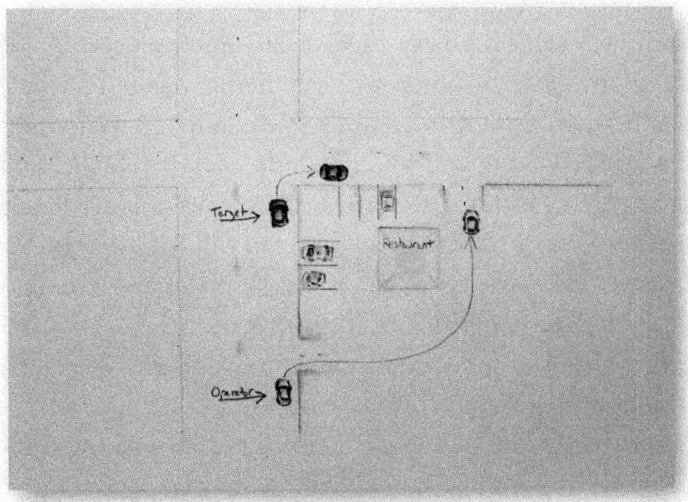

Figure 3

Maintaining a tactical distance from the subject is especially important when the subject finally arrives at his or her destination. By "tactical distance," I mean that you are in perfect position distance wise to adapt to whatever actions the subject takes. If the subject should stop in a residential community, you can easily pull over and park and continue making observations. You don't want to be so close that the subject can get a good look at you and your vehicle if he backs up to parallel park. I understand that sometimes it's unavoidable, and you end up having to drive past the subject, but whenever this happens, do not look at the subject as you drive past.

Pull over wherever possible, and monitor through your mirrors to see where the subject is going or what people he or she is engaging with. If the subject arrives at a public location, such as a shopping center with a parking lot, you want to have the time and space to enter this location through an auxiliary entrance, if possible, rather than the same one taken by the subject. You can even park in a lot across the street, if possible. This precaution is to limit your exposure as much and as often as you can. Nevertheless, tactical distance provides you with time and space to make adjustments that will keep your presence hidden so you can gather all the necessary information.

Surveilling a vehicle on the highway is somewhat easier than on the local streets in terms of not constantly being visible in your subject's rearview mirror. However, there are some challenges. What if your subject enters an HOV lane, and you are alone in your vehicle? This may be a problem for you. But apart from this, whether you are alone or with another investigator in another vehicle, you will find this part of mobile surveillance is quite manageable, especially if you are familiar with the highway you are traveling on. On the highway, the goal is to stay in your subject's blind spot or out of view entirely, which gives you a fresh start once you follow your subject off the exit.

Familiarity with the highway is helpful because if you know that all the exits are on the right side, you can just remain in the far-right lane throughout the surveillance. When your subject exits, you're already in that lane and in position to casually exit along with him or her (see figure 4). Not having to switch lanes along with the subject lessens the chance that you will be detected, especially if it is a sudden exit taken by the subject, which happens often.

Just remember to be "quiet" while on the highway. Don't change lanes frequently or speed up only to have to slow down again when there are limited vehicles on the road. If you do need to change lanes, try to do all your moves from the farthest lane and at a tactical distance, unless you are in jeopardy of losing a speedy subject. In that case, you're going to have to disregard some of your strategy until things settle down a bit. This doesn't mean you become a reckless driver on the road. Stay within the law, and do your best without getting into an accident.

One more thing about surveillance on a highway, and that is if you are surveilling a vehicle at night: try to identify if the vehicle has a unique rear-lighting signature. One night I was following a very aggressive driver on a busy highway who was not only driving fast but also bouncing from lane to lane as he navigated through traffic. Attempting to follow him by copying his moves would only expose me. What helped me to stay with him and observe him from a great distance were the unique taillights on his vehicle. Whether you're on the highway or any other road, you can also tuck in behind other vehicles or buffer cars (see figure 5) in order to hide yourself from the subject if he or she looks into his or her rearview mirror. You can at times monitor the subject through the windshield of the car in front of you. If not, you should still be able to observe through the sides of the vehicle in front of you if the subject has changed lanes or is exiting.

Here's one other thing in regards to nighttime mobile surveillance: if you have fog lights, attempt to change your appearance by alternating the light patterns coming from your vehicle. Use your usual headlights for a while, and then turn on your fog lights. Do this intermittently in order to disguise yourself.

Figure 4   Figure 5

When conducting a mobile surveillance in which more than one investigator is necessary in a separate vehicle, communication is vital for the success of the operation. Point-to-point radios, better known as walkie-talkies, and cell phones allow for this communication to take place. You should use both devices in order to take full advantage of the technology.

When multiple investigators are assigned to a surveillance, good tactics indicate that one of the investigators has a direct line of sight to the action, while the other investigator awaits instruction from a more discreet location. The moment there is action or the subject emerges, the investigator closest to the action—known as the "point"—is responsible for immediately notifying the other investigator(s). I've found that in scenarios like this, the best way to make your initial communication is through a point-to-point radio. Cell phones are great and can be used in the absence of a radio, but there is a lag time with cell phones, and things tend to happen quickly. This is opposed to the radio, which has an instantaneous connection.

The cell phone has its greatest advantage when the mobile surveillance is in motion. Often when you have multiple investigators, someone is always likely to get stuck at a traffic light, and as a result, the range for your radio is significantly decreased during this separation. This would be the time to use your cell phone in order to maintain contact with your team member(s). But remember, safety is always a priority, and a hands-free system or Bluetooth device is strongly recommended in order to be in compliance with the law and to avoid accidents.

Using both devices has another advantage, and that is that they prolong each other's battery lives. That's especially important for the cell phone because of its many other functions during a surveillance operation. You should always have a car charger; you want to have an adequately charged cell phone in the event that your mobile surveillance suddenly becomes an extended foot surveillance. Portable cell phone chargers are also handy because you never know how long your foot surveillance will last.

You should also keep your surveillance vehicle well organized for two reasons. First, you want to be able to quickly locate items or equipment that are called for at any given moment. Second, you may have to suddenly exit your vehicle and continue your surveillance on foot.

As a result, you want to be able to quickly gather the necessary equipment without delay and hide the remaining equipment that you will not be able to bring with you. You don't want to leave any equipment that will be visible to thieves or that will be evidence that reveals the reason you're in the area. Mobile surveillance offers a lot of creature comforts such as a place to sit, climate control, privacy, and good concealment for recording. But you also have some very real concerns like where to park your vehicle if you have to engage in a foot surveillance while in a high-crime neighborhood.

Another concern are the tickets you may receive as a result of a red-light infraction or speed-camera violation. Accidents are other concerns for which your employer is not likely to compensate you. So be careful when conducting mobile surveillance, and don't take unnecessary risks. While on the subject of safety, be careful when and if you are discovered. You may have done everything right, and yet your subject has detected you. This is why you should also have an exit plan in place when you think the jig is up and you feel it's time to move.

This doesn't in any way contradict what I said earlier about overcoming the paranoia that you have been detected. What I'm talking about here is a legitimate burn. I can tell you from experience that you usually get a heads-up before things go sideways. Besides avoiding detection, you especially want to avoid a car chase. So, when you exit a surveillance operation for any reason, always check to see if you're being followed. And if you are, either call the police or head straight to the precinct.

Key Points

- Follow all of your preparation, planning, and strategy procedures. If possible, determine how long it will take you to arrive at your assignment location the day before the assignment.
- Select a good surveillance vehicle with the suggested colors and free of stickers or significant damage.

- Select the proper clothing that works well with the dark interior of your surveillance vehicle.
- Tint windows with respect to the law.
- Attempt to memorize at least one car plate in relation to your subject before you arrive at the location of operation.
- Create an excuse for being in the area of operation
- Secure a good observation post.
- Park among other vehicles for better concealment.

   When confronted, do not suddenly take off unless your safety is concerned.

- Document as much as you can within reason.
- If your subject begins making erratic moves with his or her vehicle, consider increasing your distance or just let the subject go. He or she may be on to you, or worse yet, you could end up in an accident.

5

Foot Surveillance

Foot surveillance is determined by the nature of your assignment. It may even start out as a mobile surveillance that suddenly becomes a foot surveillance. You may also be directed to ride along with another investigator as a passenger in order to provide foot surveillance if necessary. Or you may have to travel to a location by public transportation because the only way to conduct your surveillance will be on foot.

Assignments that call for a strict foot surveillance are generally done in public places. A foot surveillance in a residential community with no businesses or commercial establishments you can use to deflect attention would be awkward and would expose you right away. Following someone into a residential neighborhood and acquiring an address or other information is fine, but remaining there in front of someone's home undetected is a tremendous challenge. In urban areas, it may be easier because of large multiple dwellings, but this is not so in the suburbs or rural areas.

As I stated in the previous chapter, even if you are conducting a mobile surveillance on your own, you should be aware that you may have to ditch your car and continue on foot. This is why the planning stage for your assignment is so important for both mobile and foot surveillances.

When your assignment calls for a strict foot surveillance, you have to check the weather and modify what equipment you will bring along. Bringing too much gear will be cumbersome to your task and make you stand out. Nevertheless, the essentials are required, and you have to figure out how to do this. First, begin with the weather, and determine what clothing is appropriate. Keep in mind that your clothing should be dark or neutral in color, and if it's raining, a yellow raincoat will not cut it. You should also consider clothing with multiple pockets. Many coats and jackets today have multiple pockets on the outside and inside, including the sleeves. There are even T-shirts with multiple pockets.

As far as pants are concerned, I strongly recommend cargo pants because of all the pockets and storage places they provide. During the warmer months, I always wear cargo shorts because of the diminished amount of clothing, which limits where I can store equipment. A backpack can resolve most of the storage concerns, but there is some equipment that you need right away, like your camcorder. Going into your bag to recover your camera is time-consuming and sometimes requires that you take your eyes off the subject. That being said, I also believe that backpacks are an essential item in your inventory. Like with your clothing, I recommend you get a dark bag with multiple storage compartments and one that repels snow or rain so whatever is inside will not get damaged. I have several bags of different sizes to fit the occasion, but none of them is larger than your typical school backpack.

Inside your backpack, you can store backup equipment, a portable charger, a laptop or an iPad depending on the size of your bag, a voice recorder for notes, food or snacks, and additional clothing that includes at least one hat. Hats are great because they temporarily disguise you, just like in the movies, and you can alternate between having a hat on or off, or you can alternate between multiple hats.

In reference to additional clothing, I'm not referring to pants. You need clothing you can change into right away without having to go into a bathroom. I'm talking about upper-body clothing like T-shirts, sweaters, hoodies, jackets, and maybe a coat if there is room in your bag.

Reversible outer garments are also useful, especially if each side is a different color. You can also report to your assignment with layers dressing your upper body and remove and exchange them as you operate. This is called "peeling," and I learned this from the criminal world. After committing a crime, perpetrators on foot would begin to peel off the top layers of their clothing, sometimes even turning their garments inside out if the inside was a different color, thus changing their appearance as they fled. But in this business, we are going to redeem that word "peeling" and put it to good use.

A few more things here before we get to the operational side of foot surveillance. Where I live, we have Metro Cards that allow quick access to public transportation. If you work in an area that has public transportation, this Metro Card, or anything similar, is a must-have. The person you are following is very likely to have one, and if you don't, you will have to purchase one on the spot, either from a teller or a machine. As a result, your subject will be in the wind.

When you acquire one of these cards, you should purchase multiple trips because you do not know how many trips your subject is going to make. It is also important to check the expiration on these cards; you don't want to arrive at a turnstile and discover that access is being denied because your card is expired. When you plan ahead and discover that your Metro Card is about to expire, you can merge the funds into a new card with an extended expiration. This card should be with you whenever you are conducting a surveillance, including a mobile surveillance.

There are also times when your subject will hail a cab, leaving you no choice but to do the same if you are on foot. I recommend that you always have about a hundred dollars on hand in the event that this should happen, because credit cards are too time-consuming, and every second counts.

I also recommend the use of headphones that connect to your cell phone when engaged in a foot surveillance, either hardwire or Bluetooth; the preference is up to you. This gadget is great on a foot surveillance because it blocks out a lot of the outside noise when you're in the street and assures that you will hear an incoming phone call. Now, to be clear here, the call I'm referring to is not solely one between you and your friends or loved ones; it's a call that is pertinent to your case. It may be your employer or the client who needs to impart some helpful information. Or it may be members of your team if your surveillance calls for multiple investigators.

Upon arriving at the target location, check for surveillance cameras, possible security guards, and maintenance personnel who may expose your presence. Continue your examination of the location to determine the parking situation, like if there is an underground garage or a private outdoor garage with direct access from inside the building. You also need to check on how many exits the location has so you can decide on an observation post focused on one or multiple areas of concern. Try to locate an area with the heaviest traffic for your observation post; this way, your presence is obscured. Standing in an isolated area makes you noticeable and suspicious. Be creative, and think outside the box in terms of blending in and gathering intel, and as you do this, remember to always stay within the boundaries of the law. One possible infraction is trespassing, and you could violate this accidentally if you get carried away in your surveillance and are not careful.

As you wait for your subject to emerge, remain aware of your surroundings to see if anyone has become suspicious of your presence in the area. If so, you need to move unless you have a believable story to remain in your current position. Also, glance at the windows of the target location in the event that the subject or others are looking outside and might be able to detect you. Change your location only when necessary. Your aim is always to be "quiet" by avoiding constant movement.

When your subject finally emerges, don't pop out of your position right away. Get a full description of the clothing the subject is wearing, especially the footwear, because other clothing items tend to change more frequently. Once the subject begins to move, your engagement will depend on the environment you are in. If you are in a big city like Manhattan, you can surveil the subject on the same side of the street in most areas because of the volume of people. If you decide to surveil from the same side of the street, remain behind a pedestrian or pedestrians who will shield you from the subject. However, if you're in an area with a limited number of pedestrians, I strongly suggest that you conduct your foot surveillance from the opposite side of the street (see figure 6).

Whatever strategy you employ, you must give the subject a reasonable amount of space. You don't want to be so close that if your subject suddenly stops, you end up in his or her immediate field of vision. If for some reason this does happen, casually walk past the subject with your head turned away. You must avoid eye contact and use your peripheral vision or any windows in the area to monitor his or her status. At the same time, when you follow a subject, you don't want to be too far back and miss the location he or she enters or lose him or her entirely. I've seen surveillance operators give their subjects way too much room and lose them as a result.

In less populated areas, you should surveil your subject from across the street and remain in his or her blind spot. If your subject stops for any reason, you can enter a public area that may be accessible or pretend to be going into a residence. If by chance there is nothing available for you to use to deflect suspicion, you can adjust your pace accordingly and pretend to be texting or in the middle of an animated phone conversation. You can also hide behind parked vehicles to monitor your subject through the vehicle windows. If the windows are tinted, even better, but if not, they still offer some concealment. You can also use the side-view mirror of any vehicle and pretend to be looking at your face in an attempt to locate your subject. Plainly looking back directly at your subject is something you want to avoid because you do not want to become familiar to this person.

This brings up another point that either you or others can judge for you. If you are considered an attractive individual, you need to account for this because your subject may realize this as well. You're going to need to tone it down. This should be part of your planning when selecting your surveillance attire. If your hair color or style is very distinguishable, you need to find a way to disguise that by wearing some sort of head covering. The goal as a surveillance operator is to be plain and to look like everyone else—in other words, "invisible." Any deviation from this dramatically increases the chance of you being detected.

As we continue with an active foot surveillance, I am reminded of something I learned as a police officer. When your subject turns onto a side street, avoid running up to the corner and making the turn. You can hustle up, but you must stop short of the corner and then continue in a normal pace, as if you were going to cross the street. And if conditions allow, you should cross the street and continue the surveillance from the opposite side of the street (see figure 7).

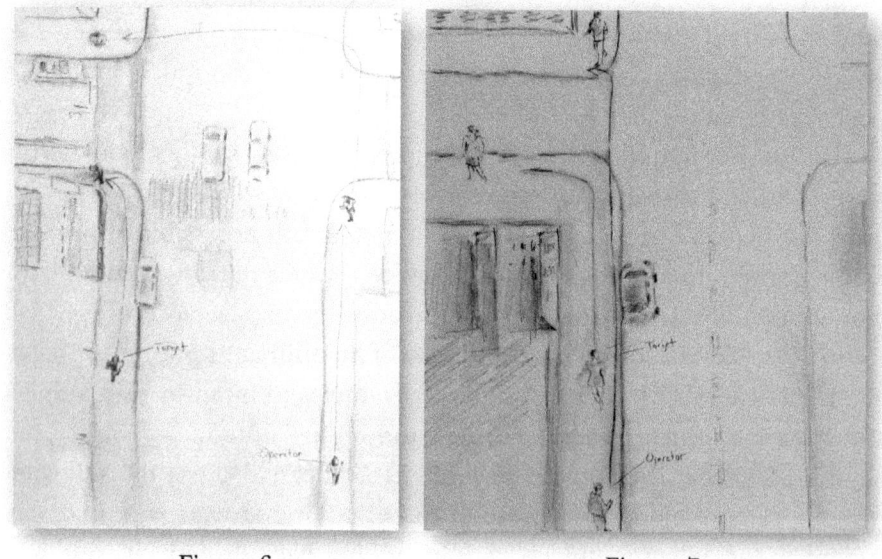

Figure 6   Figure 7

By the way, if there is a store or some other commercial establishment that has windows on both sides of the corner where your subject turned, you need to begin your casual pace sooner because the subject may be looking for you through the windows. Going around corners to see what follows is a counter-surveillance move you need to be aware of.

I became familiar with this for different reasons. When I graduated from the police academy, I was assigned to a violent and high-crime area that was not safe even for police officers. Upon arriving at my command, we were immediately lectured on how to pursue a fleeing criminal on foot. The instructors emphasized to never pursue a perpetrator stride for stride around a corner. Instead, we were instructed to run into the street and make a wide turn whenever a fleeing felon turned onto a side street. The reason for this was because in this particular area, it was a common occurrence for criminals to purposely go around a corner when chased in order to wait for the pursuing police officer to turn and then shoot him or her. That was pretty ruthless, and unfortunately that lesson was learned by a police officer the hard way. It's a lesson that has always remained with me and one that I've found very useful in the private sector.

Now let's say you lose your subject for whatever reason. Remain calm and canvass the immediate area, continuously gazing back to the area where visual sight of the subject was first lost. Things happen very fast during a surveillance, and by relaxing, you are able to slow things down so that you can think. If you are not able to locate the subject, remain in that area, because it is very likely the subject will either backtrack or emerge from some unknown location.

If after a reasonable amount of time, the subject has not returned, reassess and consider going back to the location where the subject was first picked up. It's frustrating to lose a subject, but focus on the positives, and consider what you have learned about the subject that you did not know before. You have a time that the subject first exited a location, a live look at the subject, type of clothing, direction of travel, and where and how you lost him or her during a surveillance. All these things are helpful and can lead to success—if not in your current assignment, then in future surveillances. In adding my own twist from a baseball phrase, "You are only as good or as bad as yesterday's surveillance." This ought to encourage you and humble you at the same time.

Every assignment presents its own unique challenges, and the worst thing you can do is say that an assignment you just received is going to be easy. Your surveillance can start off as a casual foot surveillance, and suddenly your subject enters the subway. This is where things get really interesting because you're in tighter quarters, and you cannot give your subject the same amount of space provided at the street level. And things tend to move even faster in this environment, so losing a subject here is easy. In the subway system, you are dealing with numerous anxious passengers with multiple destinations, resulting in multiple train platforms. Add to that the different train lines that pull up to the platform, and you can see why you need to remain close. The moment a train pulls into a station, a mob of people flock toward the train doors, and you need to determine if your subject will board or wait for the next train. And you need to be careful—sometimes subjects get confused themselves and board a train, only to jump off immediately.

I remember on one occasion following a subject who had boarded a train. The subject sat down, and the moment the sound beeped that the doors were about to close, she got up and exited the train as the doors were closing. Fortunately for me, I was standing by another door about twenty feet away and was able to slip out of the train along with her. You may be saying to yourself that that was a counter-surveillance move, and you would be right; I thought the very same thing. But what ended up happening was that she had simply boarded the wrong train. She eventually boarded the right train, and the surveillance continued for many more hours without any issues. This is why you have to remain closer than you'd prefer in this environment. And it was one of the reasons that I chose to stand instead of sitting on the train. I was aware of how quickly things happen here, and if I were sitting on that day, I would have lost the subject.

You don't always have to stand, especially if you are going to stand out in the subway car, but if you are going to sit, pick a seat next to an exit door. There have also been times when I have positioned myself in an adjacent subway car because I may have had too much exposure to the subject prior to the moment he or she got on the train. In those situations, I tend to always stand and use the reflection from the glass on the doors leading into the adjacent subway car to monitor my subject.

Let me add here that if you have additional clothing with you, even a hat, the subway is the place to alter your appearance because of your proximity to the subject. Only do this out of view of the subject. When the subject exits the train car, try to slow down or delay your exit. You want to remain as discreet as possible, realizing that oftentimes when people exit a train, they are confused and change directions multiple times. By delaying your approach, you avoid committing to one direction and then having to change directions again because the subject is now heading in the opposite direction. Once you exit the subway system, you can resume your normal surveillance routine and give your subject additional space.

The same goes for surveillance on a bus. While in the process of writing this book, I had just completed a surveillance that involved my surveilling someone on a bus, which is even tighter than a train car. Directly looking at the subject to monitor his status was out of the question. Using my peripheral vision was not possible because of all the pedestrians standing closely together, blocking my subject. So I used the windows of the bus to check on my subject and was able to see when he was ready to exit.

When your subjects are actively moving about on foot, monitor their every action closely from behind, and see if they drop something that may be considered evidence of their activity. This is known as pocket litter in the business of surveillance and can be quite helpful. Just be careful about your location when you recover the discarded item. You don't want to do this in an area where the item is still considered private property because that's illegal. If an item is dropped on a public street or in a public trash can, it becomes accessible and legal to pick up, so far as I know. But make sure, just to be on the safe side.

Recording your subject on a foot surveillance is not as comfortable as recording from the inside of your vehicle but may be necessary, depending on the nature of your case. Covert cameras are nice to have, but they cannot zoom in. Cell phones are also nice, but unless you have an app that helps with displaying the date/time stamp, which is essential in most cases, you still have to go elsewhere. The appropriate equipment for this would be the camcorder. But you have to find some sort of concealment or diversion. You can tuck into a store or restaurant, even behind another vehicle, and record through the windows. There have been times when I've given my back to the subject and placed my camera on a fixed object in order for it to record what is behind me.

While the camera is securely positioned, you can locate the subject by rotating the LCD screen on your camcorder. Once the subject has been located, you can begin recording without holding it in your hands. You can even disguise the camera by placing items around it. This technique should divert attention away from you because you are not facing the subject, but you must be a safe distance away. The zoom feature on the camcorder is what makes it possible for you to pull this off from a safe distance. What also makes this possible is if the subject is stationary or moving about in a small area. If the subject is in route to a location, this may not work. I have also created a prop, constructed from a shoe box and Styrofoam (see figures 8 and 9), in which I can place my camcorder and record from anywhere, even while moving, and no one will know what I'm doing.

Covert cameras are great tools, but you have to get very close to the subject in order to see more detail and confirm someone's identity. The decision on when to use a covert camera is determined by a couple of things. One is the condition of your surveillance. If your subject enters a location like a club or a store, you will need to use a covert camera because a camcorder would be too obvious in close quarters, although I have been able to pull this off. Length of surveillance also plays a role— but a small one. If it's a multiday surveillance, I try to hold off on the covert camera because of the exposure I will get by being close to the subject, unless the evidence needed presents itself right away. You can use a covert camera anytime because it's hidden, but it is most effective in confined areas or indoors where there are low-light conditions.

Figure 8   Figure 9

A one-day surveillance is different, and you only have one chance to get it right. That being said, if you are in a big city, taking out your camera in public isn't such a big deal. I do this all the time and even record my subjects off any window that may reflect their image if there is an issue regarding my concealment. By doing this I limit any suspicion toward me because my camera is not pointing at them. Typically, there is always a risk whenever you engage your camcorder, especially during a foot surveillance. Looking through the viewfinder of your camera in order to focus on your subject blinds you to what's going on around you. In spite of that, video recordings of your observations are crucial to the success of your case. It would be nice if our word alone were good enough, but video evidence is hard to deny.

There is other recording equipment out there that can assist you and limit your suspicion to others, but the problem with those is that many of them do not have the date/time stamp feature that is required by most employers and clients. I understand the importance of the time stamp, but it's a shame because it limits us on the equipment we can use. Nevertheless, there is still an adequate inventory for us to choose from in order to get the job done.

Key Points

- Follow all your preparation procedures.
- Check the weather forecast in order to dress appropriately.
- Downsize to the essential equipment necessary for your assignment.
- Select the right color for clothing.
- Select the right backpack.
- Carry a Metro Card.
- Carry cash.
- Canvass the area of operation for all possible exits and parking garages if necessary. Also, canvass for anything that may expose you, like surveillance cameras.
- Select a good observation post and avoid constant movement.
- Avoid trespassing.
- Avoid eye contact.
- Avoid giving your subject too much room, especially in the subway.

6

Equipment and Usage

$\mathbf{A}$ FTER THE PHYSICAL part of surveillance comes the technical side. I used to say that you're only as good as your equipment, but I have had to rethink that. There is no doubt that quality surveillance equipment makes you better in many ways, but the ability to follow someone should not be diminished regardless of what kind of equipment you have. Without the skills to properly track someone, you would not have the opportunity to use your equipment. That being said, I have done surveillance work for a long time and have done good work with borrowed and inferior equipment. As I became more involved and aware of technology that could assist me in my work, I began investing in my own equipment.

There is a vast amount of equipment available for this work, but most important to the client and your employer are the devices that produce video or at the very least, photos. That's because these images become evidence. If after testing the waters, you discover that this type of work is for you, I would suggest that you get your own equipment. By having your own equipment, you don't have to go into the office every time you get an assignment to borrow your employer's equipment, only to report back to the office to return the equipment. That takes time that you are not compensated for. If you calculate the time it takes you to go back and forth to the office for equipment, you will discover that if you had your own, it would pay itself off. Having your own equipment also allows you to freelance and work for as many PI companies as you want, and it makes you look professional.

In addition, if you have your own equipment, you will treat it better, and since you prepare before every surveillance, you will know that your equipment is charged and working properly. Equipment that is often borrowed is usually not taken care of properly or even charged correctly when handed over to you. Unfortunately, unless you are already a photographer, you are going to be confused about what video equipment to purchase, and most of your education will come from your own trials and errors. I am not a photographer either, but I will go over a couple of features that I think are the most important, along with other gadgets that are helpful in this line of work.

One more thing before we get into the equipment section. An interesting question came up while preparing this chapter, and it had to do with the issue of weapons for an investigator's safety. As you already know, I'm a retired police officer and as such I am licensed to carry a firearm. However, I rarely ever carry a weapon while doing private investigative work. And although I've had a couple of menacing moments, I thank God that it never has come to the point where I needed to use a weapon, and I've done many, many surveillances. The only reason I did arm myself for those few occasions was because I was operating in extremely high crime areas, not for protection from the subject under surveillance. For those of you who are properly licensed to carry a weapon, I leave the decision to you and your employer. I'm not going to get involved with that. You need to understand something here: the goal of a surveillance operator is to be invisible and to avoid confrontation. Even if you are approached by an irate individual, diffuse the situation, call the police, and get out. That's the best advice I can offer on this subject.

Smartphone

I want to start with the smartphone because this one device is so versatile, it is a must-have. I used to carry a flip phone and looked forward to the day when I no longer needed to carry a phone around. Now things have changed dramatically, and I don't know if I will ever be without one. When I committed to this device, I immediately discovered the advantages this tool could provide in the world of private investigations.

Any doubt that may have existed was completely eliminated after an experience I had during a strange surveillance. This is the abridged version of events. I was once directed to conduct a surveillance on a subject who was already aware he was being followed. The subject lived in a community that was surrounded by an immense wooded and hilly area. My assignment was to initiate a foot surveillance and to enter the public section of the forest from where I would conduct my surveillance. The first problem was that the client was directing this surveillance, and the information being provided was shaky. That's why I said earlier that clients should never direct surveillances.

Anyway, let's get to the point here. An event occurred that prevented me from returning the way I had entered the forest and to where my vehicle was without being detected. I had to find another way and soon learned I was lost in the forest. I thought about the map feature on my phone and was able to discover a road farther along in the forest. Eventually I was able to get out of the forest and back to my vehicle with a new appreciation for this device.

The smartphone also provides a navigational feature in the form of a GPS, along with a large selection of apps that can assist you in this field of work. The following is a list of some of the apps I use and a brief description:

- Google Maps shows you a satellite view of your location of interest and allows you to navigate the neighborhood you're going to be working in from a remote location. I also use this app to take screenshots of pertinent locations in either satellite or map mode. I have also used it to acquire the unknown address of a location.

- NYC Subway provides a map of the entire subway system, including the individual lines and stops the train makes. This is also helpful in determining where a subject may arrive or depart from. This is what we have in New York, but I'm sure there's one for your area as well.
- FlightView provides information on plane arrivals and departures.
- Spoof Card allows you to disguise the number you are calling from as well as your voice.
- Burner works like a burner phone, except it's an app.
- Waze advises you as to where speed and traffic-light cameras may be located.
- Theodolite is a unique camera app that provides a lot of information when you take a photo. I believe this app is also used by surveyors.
- Evernote is a note-taking app. I don't really use it because of other resources I have. But it's an app that appears to be popular with investigators who use it for taking notes.
- Winmail Viewer and Letter Opener are both helpful when an e-mailed assignment is refusing to open on your end. You can view both text documents and photos.

Photo Apps

There are numerous photo apps to choose from, but I've found that the standard photo app that comes with the phone can just about do it all. With the photo app, I can take pictures of anything, including the subject. I can zoom in or put the phone to my ear when I'm within close proximity to the subject and use the burst feature to take multiple random photos instead of aiming the phone, which would make it too obvious.

Just one warning here, though: make sure you turn off the flash and the sound the phone makes when taking photos. Not doing those things can really spoil your investigation.

You can also record with the phone and either e-mail or text-message the video or photos to your employer or the client instantly. On many occasions, I've also recorded or taken photos of the LCD screen on my camcorder that display subjects or other things of relevance. I then e-mail or text the captured media to the proper source in order to confirm the identity of someone under surveillance or to verify other information. The smartphone also has a voice recorder, which can be useful in taking notes or when trying to quickly document a plate number or address when you're on foot and writing doesn't seem appropriate.

And last but not least is an app that I mentioned before but haven't decided whether I will publish it or not. I have a name for the app but will refrain from revealing it here until I can be assured I can use it. At some point, I will let the readers know on my website if and when the app will be published. In a nutshell, the app was designed as a tool for surveillance investigators but can be used by process servers and the general public as well because of its interesting functionality. The app allows you to document multiple locations on a map relating to a specific case. Seeing these locations marked on a map all at once gives you an idea of the places your subjects frequent and could assist you in locating them if you lose them in the vicinity of the documented locations.

The app also enables you to have your colleague(s) join your map and share all the information already documented, including the locations of those invited into the map. This gives you the opportunity to strategize and reposition yourselves according to what is visible on the map and the location of your subject.

Moving along, I would also recommend you get a portable charger for your phone because there will be times when your phone will need a boost during a long foot surveillance.

Finally, my phone is the device that I get all my assignments from. Employers contact me by e-mail and send me the assignment along with any available photos. I save all the information and can recall it at any time without having to carry documents that can easily be lost. I've spent a lot of time on this one piece of equipment, but I wanted to show you how important and useful it is in making your job easier.

Camcorder

This device documents and gathers vital information related to your case, so it is important to have a good camcorder. I won't get into name brands, but you can go online and search for the most reliable ones out there. Unless you are a skilled photographer, you are not going to be able to tell the difference, but here are some of the things I would look for. Does the camera have a decent amount of zoom? The better the zoom, the farther away you can be to make your observations. Does it have an SD card slot along with internal memory? Some cameras only have the one feature. I prefer both because it gives me more options. Having the SD card capability allows me to just hand over the video to my employer or client upon completion, and no uploading is necessary on my part. Also, the time-stamp feature is important. This is a visual display of the date and time of the recording on your video. This is an essential element of evidence that also proves your presence at the location of operation even when nothing is happening.

Whenever I arrive at an assignment, I attempt to capture a clear recording of the location, and if possible, I pan the camera to the nearest street sign in one continuous video shot. You can also record street signs when the dynamics of the neighborhood prevent you from setting up an observation post within view of the target location. I do this to dispel any doubt as to the time and the location where I am operating. When recording, you must be aware of your surroundings the moment you engage your camera to record something.

Not all companies do this, but the ones I work for require something called a "time shot." A time shot is when you take an hourly recording, in some cases every half hour, of the location under surveillance to demonstrate you are still present. I understand the reasoning behind this, but every time that camera comes up to eye level, you are taking a risk of being exposed. Due to the current conditions in the world we live in, people tend to have a heightened awareness of their surroundings, especially when it comes to children (as it should be). So you need to be even more careful when filming in an area where there are children, because that can quickly lead to a confrontation.

You need to account for everything, including the size of your camcorder. I have two camcorders, but I prefer the smaller one because it is very portable. Another thing I should mention about camcorders is that they also take photos and from my experience eliminate the need for the traditional camera. With today's camcorders, you can either take a photo or pause the video you took and snap a photo of the desired image.

As far as low-light recording is concerned, the camcorder has its limits in this area. On my camcorders, I have two features: "color night mode" and "infrared night mode." Color night mode works great in low-light settings, but the second something moves—like the subject, a passing vehicle, or the unsteadiness of your own hand—the image becomes distorted until there is some stability on both sides of the camera. The infrared night mode is good but only up to about fifty feet, so you have to be pretty close to your subject.

There isn't much else you can do about nighttime shooting unless you have the money to buy the really expensive stuff or you improvise. Depending again on the geographical location of the surveillance, I have at times turned on my headlights in the direction of the subject when filming at night and when doing so would not expose me. The other thing you can do is to get a monopod or tripod for your camera. I have found this greatly improves the image quality I'm trying to capture at night, using the color night mode, because it stabilizes the camera.

One more tip here before moving on: I always carry a seat cushion (see figure 10) that has a cutout in it (for added comfort, I imagine). Nevertheless, I use this seat cushion all the time because it blocks any light coming from the camera and completely blocks me from view, allowing me to capture video through the cutout just feet away from my subjects. The videos and photos I capture using this device are so stunning that it makes it look as if the subjects are staring at me while I film them.

Figure 10

GPS

Although many cell phones today have GPS, I still use a stand-alone GPS for surveillance. I prefer it that way because it also preserves the battery on my phone. Nevertheless, the ability to use both devices is also an advantage. I have a stand-alone GPS that is voice activated and is useful if I'm driving because I can just speak to it and get results without having to pull over to input the information. It also prevents me from taking my eyes off the road for an extended period.

Body-Worn Covert Camera

There is a whole array of covert cameras on the market, and selecting one will require patience, trial, and error. Many of these devices are delicate, with small buttons next to other small buttons in tight places. You have to consider your style and what you feel comfortable using. For surveillance purposes, you need a "body-worn covert camera." These come in many forms, such as a button or pinhole spy camera, a car remote, a Bluetooth headset, spyglasses, watches, hats, and the list goes on. These are all useful, but what separates all of these cameras is their low-light capability.

I use a button camera with low-light proficiency that connects to a mini portable DVR because the other devices do not work well in low-light conditions. The button, or pinhole, camera operates with a mini portable DVR. The camera part of the button-camera system is the small device with a wire that connects to the mini DVR (see figure 11). It can be cumbersome because of the wires, but you can't argue with its effectiveness.

You can also dedicate clothing you are comfortable with and redesign it to work with your covert camera. I have a jacket with a button sewn on the left side and an eyelet sewn on the right side where I can install the button camera (to see a side-by-side comparison, see figures 12 and 13). You cannot see the difference at all.

Another reason to consider using a covert camera is for when, or if, you're serving subpoenas. I know the focus here is surveillance, but there may be times when you will be asked to serve a subpoena. This part of private investigations can present some problems because people do not like getting served and may in turn make a false allegation against you. The covert camera is a way to protect yourself in the event someone makes a false claim. Audio is not always necessary, and you need to know the laws in your state. You don't want to record someone's voice in a two-party state. A two-party state means that in that state, consent is needed by every person in the conversation you are recording.

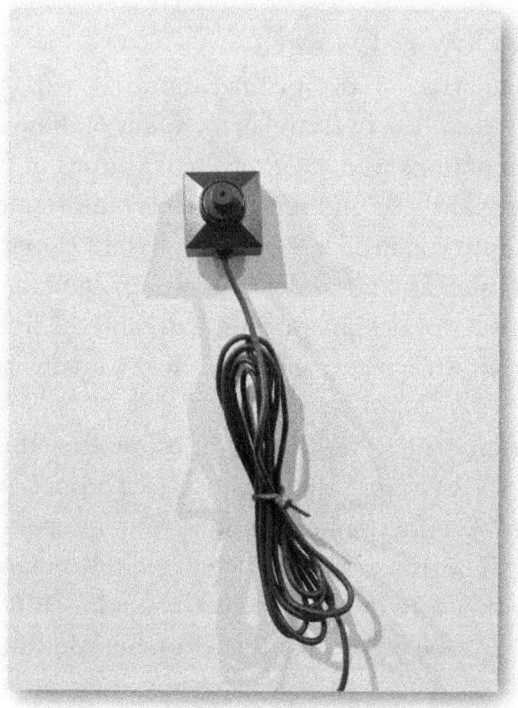

Figure 11

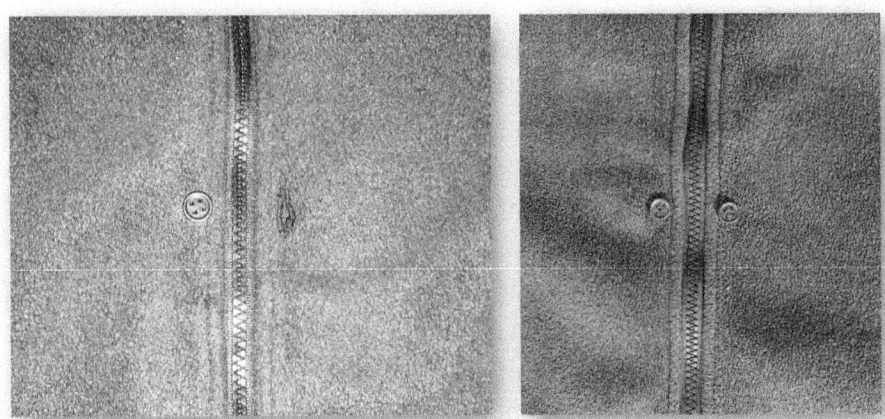

Figure 12   Figure 13

Laptop or Tablet

Having a laptop or tablet in the field provides some key benefits. It allows you to prepare your notes in an organized manner, which ends up saving you additional time spent writing a report for which you will not be compensated. It also provides the means to save all your cases and related photos in one device in the event you need to do research on a case you've been working on for a while.

Dash Cam

This device is attached to either your dashboard or windshield for the sole purpose of recording everything in front of you. I'm not a big fan of these, but if you're in the market for one, I would recommend one that works well in low-light conditions. And like the covert camera, there is no zoom, so you have to be close. Make sure you get one with date/time stamp capability. If you can't afford to buy one or are curious about the results they may provide, you can experiment with your camcorder. All you would need is one of those suction cups that can be attached to your dashboard or windshield. I've done this when the possibility of something important occurring very quickly was evident and holding a camera with my hands would not be a good idea. The good thing about using a camcorder this way is that it has zoom capability, unlike your common dash cams. There are also some nice action cameras in the market that take great videos and photos and can be voice activated. Nevertheless, among some of the issues mentioned earlier concerning covert cameras is that I haven't seen one with the all-important date/time stamp feature. And that right there can be a deal breaker for some.

Time-Lapse Camera

Some camcorders and even covert cameras have a time-lapse feature. The problem with using this feature exclusively on the devices just mentioned is that it will wear your battery and consume valuable time when you need to use those devices for other things. If you can afford it, a dedicated time-lapse camera is a good item to have. You can park your car close to the target location, disguise your camera by creating a box for it, and exit your vehicle while your camera does all the work. No one will be too concerned because the car is unoccupied.

I have used this feature when it was absolutely necessary to capture a subject as he or she was exiting a specific door. A subject may be in a location for hours, and a holding a camcorder for that amount of time may not capture the image necessary for your case. Plus, the camcorder takes a few seconds to be ready to record once you open the LCD door. With a time-lapse camera, all you have to do is set it and forget it.

Backpack

Backpacks are great because they allow you to blend in with everyone else while you carry all your important equipment. Even if you are conducting a mobile surveillance, a backpack is necessary because you may have to exit your car to continue the surveillance on foot. This is all part of your preparation. You need a bag with multiple pockets or compartments so you can store your devices in an organized manner. You don't want things thrown all around in your bag; you want to be able to locate an item quickly when you need it. Furthermore, these delicate surveillance devices can get damaged when not secured properly.

When selecting a bag, decide if you are going to be carrying a laptop or a tablet because some bags cannot support the size of a laptop. I have the following bags for different settings: a traditional school backpack, a sling bag, and a messenger bag. When I know that I will be on a lengthy foot surveillance and cannot bring all my equipment, I downsize and bring a tablet instead. You can even you use the proper app on your smartphone to take down notes for your report if space is a major issue.

Power Inverter

All these devices you carry for surveillance have one thing in common: they all need to be charged. A power inverter can recharge multiple devices at once depending on the one you purchase, and power inverters are not limited to the typical AC outlets. Some power inverters even have USB slots and cigarette-lighter slots. There is a whole assortment of these, and they are not expensive.

Flashlight

Flashlights are always good to have. I have a couple and one that produces a red light. Arguably, the red light may be a little more discreet and supposedly preserves your night vision.

Portable Car-Jump Starter

This is a must-have for mobile surveillance. There will be times when you accidentally leave something on in your vehicle, and your battery dies. In a situation like this, you will wish you had one of these. So much goes on during a surveillance that sometimes things slip by. On several occasions, I've had my car battery die, but in all my situations, I was blessed to have a way out because I didn't have a portable jump starter at the time. In one case, it was late in the evening, and I was a long way from home. I had charging cables and was able to get some assistance from another motorist, but my vehicle would not take the charge. The motorist was about to give up when a kind neighbor who saw my predicament came out with a portable car charger, and within seconds, my car sprang to life.

I was so impressed that I not only bought one for myself but also for my whole family. Some of them can be expensive but provide other services as well like a compressor to fill your tires, a light to illuminate the work area, and the ability to charge your electronic devices—not to mention the money it would save you if otherwise you had to call in for assistance and have your car towed.

Mobile Hotspot Device

This device allows you to wirelessly connect devices that are Wi-Fi enabled to the Internet. I use this whenever there is some discrepancy as to the identity of a subject that needs to be identified and the image taken by cell phone of my camcorder LCD screen may not be clear enough. After taking video of one or more possible subjects, I isolate their images and upload them to my laptop while I'm in the field. I then e-mail the images to the proper channels to get an ID confirmation. Images sent in this manner are much clearer and sharper. You can also send reports from the field and receive other pertinent information that can assist you in your investigation. There is a monthly fee attached to this device that you must also consider.

Headphones

When stationary during a mobile surveillance, having headphones that can be connected via Bluetooth to either your phone or your vehicle is a good idea because it eliminates any noise coming from inside your vehicle. Depending on the volume necessary for you to hear, your car radio can be heard from outside the vehicle. Voice conversations and a ringing phone can also be heard outside a vehicle when you're using Bluetooth. At the same time, headphones should not be used while the vehicle is in motion.

I also recommend using headphones that connect to your phone, wireless or otherwise, whenever you're on a foot surveillance. In this situation, the headphones eliminate most of the outside noise and give you a better chance of being alerted to an incoming call. You can also use them to communicate with other team members who are in the field with you, and you look perfectly normal because many other pedestrians are wearing the same thing.

Glass Cleaner

Always have a bottle of glass cleaner in your vehicle to clean your car windows.

Hand Sanitizer

You use a lot of public bathrooms in this business, and the need to sanitize your hands is important to your health and to the health of others.

Car Magnets

I don't use these, but many other investigators do. They simply make up the name of an occupation they feel comfortable representing and have magnetic car decals made up to attach to the sides of their vehicles when setting up an observation post in a residential neighborhood. The cool thing about this is that you can easily remove them whenever you want to change your appearance. But the most important thing to remember is that you cannot take on the name of an already established company. You must make up the name, just like when creating a fake ID.

Clothing

We went over this before, but it's important enough to go over it again. Being "quiet" physically is just as important as being quiet audibly. You want to look like everyone else and not stand out. Wear clothing that fits your environment, and use neutral colors. This includes your footwear.

Many times I have followed individuals who blend in well with the environment and would be difficult to monitor—had they not been wearing neon-colored sneakers. Bright colors make you stick out, and it's good when subjects do this but not investigators.

Also, wear items with plenty of storage spaces that allow you to secure essential items and devices when on foot. This includes hats—not just one hat, but multiple hats—that can alter your appearance. Sunglasses are also helpful but not throughout an entire surveillance when you may have been in the subject's field of vision multiple times. Alternate your eyewear and hat combination to throw off your target.

Glow-in-the-Dark Stickers and Stage Tape

You can use these items when you are in a very dark setting and need a reference point to identify a fixed location, like the residence of your subject. Stick one of these items to a rock or the side of a tree to monitor the location from a distance.

Infrared Transmitter

This is another small, battery-operated device that can be used in dark settings to assist in giving you a reference point on a fixed target location. It cannot, however, be seen with the naked eye; you would need a night-vision device to see its illumination.

Label Machine

This isn't an absolute necessity, but with the accumulation of equipment and wires, labeling each one would not be a bad idea. It also helps in avoiding confusion between your equipment and another investigator's when working together.

Dazzle

This device is essential when you are required to produce a copy of your video recordings. Even though your recording displays the date/time stamp feature, such information may not be transferred over to a CD. You would need a device like the Dazzle to not only capture the video but also the time-stamp information.

Ziplock Bags

These are great to organize your device wires. Mixing wires together in a confined area tangles them up and makes things more difficult when needed.

Drones

I'm mentioning this piece of equipment because I'm sure many are curious about it. Drones, or UAS, are interesting; however, you need to be aware of all the regulations regarding recreational and commercial use. I have limited knowledge in this area because the situation has been fluid for a while. Currently, as I understand the situation, you need to acquire a remote pilot license if you're going to use a drone for commercial reasons. The exam for this license is called, The FAA Part 107 Aeronautical Knowledge Test. They have significantly reduced the requirements from its previous state. However, my advice would be to stay away from this piece of equipment until you fully understand the requirements and how to use it properly without breaking the law. The fines are severe.

This completes my immediate list of items, but there's plenty of room for you to add more. One more thing I'd like to mention: try to purchase all your devices in black because they more discreet, especially at night.

7

Report Writing

A WRITTEN REPORT IS necessary for every surveillance. If you are working on a case that requires multiple days of surveillance, an individual report for each day of surveillance is recommended. You or your employer can provide the client with a supplemental or summary report at the end of the investigation, but daily reports are easier and convenient to follow.

Try to complete your report right after each surveillance, while the information is still fresh in your mind. Delaying or allowing unfinished reports to accumulate during other surveillances only causes confusion of the details. Your report should be grammatically accurate and free from any assumptions and embellishments. Present only the facts as you observed them, regardless of the outcome.

The surveillance reports I prepare follow a timeline, and it's important that your video recordings correspond with the documented times on your report. Most of my reports are documented with military time; very few employers that I've come across prefer civilian time. In my reports, I never document my full name, only my initials. I also write my reports in the third person so that it appears as if someone else is writing it, making my identity ambiguous to anyone on the opposing side who may read it for whatever reason. I understand that an employer may be required to reveal the name of the investigator if the case goes to trial or a hearing, but I continue to write them in this manner regardless. Your report should also be articulate, with as much reasonable detail as possible. Small details can lead to important clues and even the solution to your investigation.

Upon arriving at your assignment, take a quick video of the location. Then begin to document a detailed description of your findings. Is it a residential building? If so, is it a one-family or two-family home? Were the lights on or off when you arrived? Is it a brick or wood frame structure? What's the color of the domain? How is it designed? Is there a porch or garage? Is the type of community residential or commercial? How many vehicles are parked at the location?

If it's a private home, record the license plate numbers of the vehicles on the property. Are there garbage cans at the end of the driveway (an indicator that someone has been at this location recently)? I remember showing up early to a location on a snowy day; I could tell there had already been activity and the direction of that activity because of the tire tracks on the snow leading out of the driveway. Also, take mental notes of the activity of the neighborhood, such as who's going or coming from work, who's going to school, who's walking the dogs, and at what time these things are occurring. This can be helpful to you or another investigator who conducts a follow-up surveillance and is searching for a good observation post.

When trying to point out the location of something being described, some use the terms left side, right side, front, or rear, but it is only relative from their perspective. Let me explain. If you are facing a house from the outside and describe an attached garage on the left side of the house, that location would be on the right side of the house from someone inside. To remedy this, some investigators use cardinal or compass directions: north, south, east, and west. The fact that these points are fixed makes this method the most accurate course to take in providing proper orientation for the reader.

Sometimes in a surveillance, you have numerous active players who may be known or unknown; referring to one as "the tall Caucasian male with the down coat," for example, is not the most expedient way to document in your report every time this individual does something. What you can do here is look for a specific characteristic of the individual that helps in making him or her identifiable, and add the initials JD—for John Doe or Jane Doe—before that characteristic. So if your player has a noticeable scar on his or her face, you can document this person on your report as "JD-Scar" or "JD-Scarface." This is a placeholder name until you can identify or eliminate him or her from your investigation. When referring to your subject, you can refer to the individual as the subject, target, or by the subject's last name. It depends on the policy of the agency you work for.

Essential to my reports is something called a "time shot." These are video shots taken every hour, especially if you've been sitting at the same location for a while waiting for something to happen. This helps to prove that you were present and did not leave the location. If your subject is active and moving about, it isn't so important to record every hour because you're probably recording the subject's activities. It's also not that important that the recording be made exactly on the hour; just try to keep it close. At the same time, don't force yourself to take a time shot if people are near you. They may see you. Just wait for them to leave and explain it in your report if necessary. Equally as important is that you also record the time of your arrival and departure.

One last thing here about reports. Some PI companies put a limit on how much time you can bill a client for your report. After a surveillance, it can easily take you up to two hours to organize your notes and match them to your video. If your employer imposes a limit of, say, one hour, and it took you longer to do it, you will not get compensated for that extra time. To avoid this, I write my draft on my computer or tablet while I'm in the field. This way, when I get home, all I have to do is make corrections and add other details rather than starting from scratch. Sometimes I still go over the allotted time but not by much and not often. If you're good with your computer, you can even add photos to your reports that illustrate places and persons of interest. But this is not always necessary because you would also have video taken from your recording devices. Save all your reports for future references and in the event your investigation goes to trial. Below you will find an example of a surveillance report.

Surveillance Report Sample

Case #
Investigator: J.R.
Weather: 50°
January 1, 1980

0400 hrs. The investigator is in route to XXXX Street in XXXX, NY.

0445 hrs. The investigator arrives at the above-mentioned location and discovers a one-story ranch with gray vinyl siding and black shutters. The main entrance door is black and located at the center of the residence. Over the main entrance is an overhang supported by two stone pillars, gray in color. At the east end of the home is a driveway that leads to a detached two-car garage with large black doors that swing outward for vehicle access. In the driveway, the investigator observed a gray XXXXX, NY registration #11111, that is registered to the subject. Parked in front of the residence was a XXXXX SUV, PA registration #11111. Video taken.

0500 hrs. The investigator contacts the 1st Precinct and informs them of his presence in the area.

0510 hrs. The investigator observes a light come on from inside the residence.

0600 hrs. No activity to report at this time. Video taken.

0615 hrs. The investigator observes a Caucasian male, approximately 6'1", 200 pounds, salt-and-pepper hair, wearing prescription glasses, green hooded sweatshirt, blue jeans, and white sneakers, as he exits the residence and enters his gray vehicle. The male fits the description of the subject that was provided in the assignment details. Moving surveillance initiated. Video taken.

0645 hrs. The subject stops at a deli located at XXXX Street. Video taken.

0650 hrs. The subject, whose identity is confirmed at this time, exits the location with purchased items, enters his vehicle, and exits the location. Moving surveillance resumed. Video taken.

0655 hrs. The investigator notes that the subject is an erratic and aggressive driver who neglects to use his directional signals when changing lanes or making turns at intersections.

0730 hrs. The subject arrives at his workplace, located at XXXX Street. The location is a four-story commercial building constructed in red brick with large blacked-out windows throughout. The location is equipped with a keyless access card system and surveillance cameras throughout the perimeter. A security guard was observed at the main entrance. Video taken.

0800 hrs. No activity to report at this time. Video taken.

0815 hrs. The security guard is observed conducting a perimeter patrol.

0825 hrs. Mail carrier arrives to deliver mail.

0900 hrs. No activity to report at this time. Video taken.

0916 hrs. The investigator observes the subject emerge from the location to smoke a cigarette. Moments later, the subject approaches a white vehicle, NJ registration #0000, that just arrived and parked around the corner from the location. The subject had a brief conversation with the lone occupant of the vehicle before handing this individual an unknown object. Upon completion, the subject returned to his workplace. Video taken.

1200 hrs. The investigator observes the subject exit his workplace and continue on foot past his vehicle. Investigator J.R. initiates a foot surveillance. Video taken of subject as he exited the location.

1203 hrs. The investigator activates his covert camera.

1210 hrs. The subject entered a restaurant located at XXXX Street. As the investigator crossed the street to enter the same location, he observed the same white vehicle mentioned above as it arrived and parked in front of the restaurant. Seconds later, the operator, a Caucasian male, approximately 5'10", 190 pounds, shaved head, earring in the right ear, blue long-sleeve T-shirt, blue jeans, and black sneakers, exits the vehicle and enters the restaurant. This individual will be referred to as "JD-Earring" until he can be identified. Covert video taken.

1212 hrs. The investigator enters the location and observes the subject and JD-Earring sitting in an isolated area at the rear of the restaurant. Their conversation, although animated at times, is conducted in a low tone. Covert video taken.

1240 hrs. The subject is observed paying for their meals but remained seated at the restaurant. Covert video taken.

1250 hrs. The investigator observed as JD-Earring goes to the restroom. Seconds later the subject exits the location without waiting for JD-Earring to return. Moving surveillance resumed. Covert video taken.

1300 hrs. The subject returns to his workplace. Covert video taken.

1302 hrs. The investigator returns to his surveillance vehicle and continues to monitor the location. Covert video deactivated.

1600 hrs. The investigator observes the subject as he exits his workplace and enters his vehicle. Moving surveillance resumed as the subject exits the location in his vehicle. Video taken.

1602 hrs. The subject pulls over several blocks away from his workplace, exits his vehicle, places an unknown item in the trunk, and then continues in his vehicle. Moving surveillance resumed. Video taken.

1700 hrs. The subject arrives at his residence. The subject retrieves an unknown item from the trunk of his car and proceeds directly to his garage. The subject remained hidden inside his garage for several minutes before emerging to collect mail from his mailbox and then entered his home. Video taken.

1730 hrs. No further activity to report at the time. Surveillance terminated. Video taken.

Key Points

- Write a detailed report.
- Write it in the third person.
- Report only the facts. Do not make assumptions or embellishments.
- Use cardinal or compass directions for accurate placement.
- Use placeholder names when you have single or multiple players in an investigation whose identities are initially unknown.
- Take hourly "time shots" while on surveillance, especially of your arrival and departure times.
- Learn to start your reports in the field in order to save time, but not at the expense of missing something you should be watching. Your observations take precedence over any concerns about how long it will take you to complete a report.

8

A Word to Employees

U P TO THIS point, I've spoken a lot about the many aspects involved with the operations of a surveillance. But there are other things you need to be made aware of that include the business end as well. Forgive me for being blunt here, but some PI companies lack a moral compass, and their unscrupulous practices may leave you holding the bag. You don't have to be licensed to do investigative work so long as you are working for a licensed private investigator; at least, that's the way it works in New York. But if you do have a license and are working for some shady players, and a client or the subject of a case makes allegations against you, you could be open to liabilities or even the loss of your license if you signed on as an independent contractor.

So you may want to take some precautions in protecting yourself and your license and do a little research into the proper hiring practices in your locale and even the company you're thinking of working for. Many in this business have experienced, or at least have heard, of instances where the owner of a PI company has delayed payment to an investigator. This is a common problem that you need to avoid if possible. Most of the time you will get your money, but the frustration that comes with waiting to get paid is not worth it. The way it's supposed to work is that a client, seeking a particular service, provides the PI company with a retainer before any work is done. This secures payment to the company, as well as the investigator, if for any reason the client does not pay for services rendered. Work that would exceed the retainer amount should not be done until additional funds are added.

If the PI company doesn't take a retainer, and the client refuses or delays payment, you're in a predicament along with the company, and that shouldn't be your problem. I once had to report a PI to the Department of Labor in order to get a significant amount of money I was owed. I eventually won, but it took a year for me to get paid.

In my experience, late payment is more likely to occur when the PI company you're working for does a lot of insurance work. Insurance companies are slow to submit payments, and to my knowledge, retainers are not a common practice in this relationship, so you get paid when your employer gets paid.

On the subject of money, the pay rate for an investigator who works for a PI company can range from approximately fourteen dollars to sixty-five dollars an hour. Typically, someone with law-enforcement experience commands around twenty-five dollars an hour, at the very least. This base of twenty-five dollars an hour for law enforcement has been in effect for a long time and needs to be increased. PI companies are getting around four times more than the hired investigator and sometimes even more than that. I understand that the hiring company has a overhead to consider, but I'm sure there is something that can be done for the hired investigator, especially a good one.

As a hired investigator, or independent contractor, you also get paid for mileage when you use your own vehicle. How much you get paid for each mile varies among companies, as well as where you begin to document your mileage. Usually companies also pay you for your travel time, but that also varies between companies. Some compensate you from your home and back, while others pick a location where you begin to document the start time and mileage on your odometer. All of your expenses such as tolls, public transportation, parking, food for cover at a restaurant, and so on should be covered by your employer.

It is also common practice that if you arrive at a location and the surveillance is canceled or even resolved right away, you should be compensated for a minimum of three to four hours. This may not be the case if you work for one of those companies that exclusively do large volumes of insurance work. For this type of company that I'm talking about, you're very likely to be on salary, so you won't be entitled to a minimum payout; you'll probably just be sent to the next case. These companies also tend to pay less but do include most of the benefits mentioned above.

Always try to use cash in order to avoid leaving a trail by using a credit card. You may be at a restaurant, for example, and your subject has become suspicious of you and happens to know someone at the restaurant who can provide your credit card information. You want to limit a subject's opportunity to identify you. Also, always save your receipts for reimbursements.

There will be times when a PI company is inundated with surveillance work and other times when they hit a prolonged dry season. During the dry season, you're going to feel like you're glued to your phone or computer waiting for an assignment. It's an uncomfortable feeling and no way to spend your downtime. That's why it's a good idea to work for more than one company so that you can supplement your income, especially if you need to bring home a base amount every month. This work offers a lot of flexibility, but once you go operational, you cannot be certain when you'll get home.

When you do get an assignment, ask lots of questions, especially in the beginning. Oftentimes there is additional information lingering around that you weren't made aware of for whatever reason. The more information you have, the better equipped you are to understand the situation and bring it to a conclusion. In time, as you acquire more experience with each surveillance, your questions will get better and more precise. You are also going to have to protect yourself in this business and learn when to say no.

In the beginning, it will be difficult as you break into this field of work, but you are going to have to set boundaries for yourself. There will be times when you will be asked to do things that are uncomfortable, like doing a surveillance very near to your home. You should avoid this situation because if your surveillance goes bad, you now have to live near someone who is not very happy with you. There are other situations where it won't be easy to say no, but you're just going to have to learn to do it.

When I was an undercover in narcotics, I never said no to any case because I loved the work. After a while, I developed a lot of equity, so when this one particular case was offered to me, I felt like I had already arrived at a point where I didn't have to prove myself. The scene was dramatic, much like in the movies. On this day, I was doing a favor for another narcotics team, not my own, as we traveled to an isolated location on a cold, dark night. If memory serves me correctly, it was also raining. Upon arriving at our destination, a confidential informant (CI) jumped in the back seat where I was sitting. Now, I never liked working with CIs, but the flags went up immediately the moment this guy entered the vehicle. I didn't like his hubris or how the supervisor was handling the situation either, so I excused myself from the case. I hated doing it, but I had to because my gut and experience were telling me something wasn't right. I also learned that I was maturing in my role and taking responsibility for my own safety.

Learn as much as you can from more experienced investigators, and develop a style you're comfortable with. Avoid imitating step for step what other investigators are doing; your ideas or style may be better. You can also educate yourself in this business by listening to investigative topics on a podcast or by looking them up on YouTube. All you have to do is a Google search on words like "investigator," "investigative tips," or "surveillance investigations," and suddenly you'll have a whole bunch of videos to watch. You can even google "mistakes private investigators make," and you will see advice about things you should not do during a surveillance. While you're at it, google "counter surveillance." This will show you what your subjects may do to identify you.

The Internet is also full of articles that can help you improve your craft. You can also subscribe to private investigative magazines and go to seminars that are in line with your interests and specialties. Once you've decided that you like this work and it fits who you are, the goal should be to become the very best, but do not become arrogant while you're at it. Be understanding of others and willing to listen, learn, and even teach. There will always be opportunities for you to learn something new in this business. Even after all these years, I still learn something new whenever I go out on a surveillance. A good way to embark on your career would be to invest in acquiring your own equipment. And always remember to be professional and humble.

9

A Word to Employers

Acquiring good investigators will be a challenge for you, especially when it comes to good surveillance operators. Unless you've done a fair amount of surveillance yourself, you're going to need at least one to two good surveillance operators to train future investigators in your company. Word-of-mouth recommendations are always welcome but don't always pan out. It's going to be a lengthy process as you filter through many individuals who express interest in the surveillance field. Some will quickly realize that this isn't for them, and others will have to be told.

When you begin your search, don't focus only on former or current law-enforcement officers. Look for any individual who has a teachable spirit, passion, and the proper work ethic to do this work. Avoid gender bias in a field that is overpopulated by males. A good female surveillance investigator is a tremendous asset to any investigative company, and there are some really good ones out there.

Send your candidates out into the field alongside another, more seasoned investigator, and observe their reactions. Once you're comfortable with the idea of sending the new candidate out alone, give him or her manageable assignments at first so they can get their feet wet. Don't give them anything too difficult right away; otherwise, you will destroy their confidence if they fail badly. Continue sending them out there on their own because it's the only way you will know if they have any potential. Sending them out with other investigators will only mask their true abilities or inabilities. Plus, the new investigators need to be out there on their own for their own development. The pressure to succeed enables them to think on their own instead of relying on someone else. You should be able to learn quickly if your candidate has the potential you're looking for.

If it turns out that this individual doesn't have what it takes, consider what other skills he or she may have that can be useful to your company. It may be that this person needs more human interaction and is more effective at taking witness statements or handing out subpoenas instead of sitting in a car for hours, waiting for something to happen. If it turns out that this individual has nothing to offer in terms of making your company better, then cut off ties immediately. Having this person linger around is counterproductive, especially if there is an attitude problem, which can affect the rest of your team.

When you do send out an investigator on a surveillance assignment, make sure you provide all the information you have. Don't hold back facts like "the subject has been followed before and detected the surveillance team," "the subject is a police officer," "the subject is an ex-con," "the subject is known to be violent," and so on. And don't instruct investigators to do something you would not be willing to do yourself. Sometimes PI companies ask investigators to do some of the most outrageous things that don't even make sense. We all want to do a good job and satisfy the clients, but we need to check ourselves and be reasonable. Continually asking investigators to do such things will only frustrate them and cause them to distrust the leadership, and it will reflect in their work performance.

Also, avoid micromanaging. If you have any experience doing surveillance in the private sector, I understand and appreciate your unique insight. Nevertheless, if you have reliable and accomplished investigators, allow them to do their thing without always second-guessing their decisions. On the other hand, if you don't have surveillance experience, there is no way you can understand what a surveillance investigator does or encounters in the field—unless, of course, you have an investigator with a history of consistent inadequacy. In that case, it is no longer that investigator's fault but yours for maintaining this individual in your employment.

Please understand that I'm not telling you how to run your company; I'm only offering my opinion and advice. I don't encourage poor work performance that is done deliberately out of retaliation, but in my experience this is likely to happen. I have worked with many individuals in this field and have witnessed many of the behaviors and heard all the chatter that goes on between investigators. If you're fortunate enough to have good investigators, do everything possible to keep them. Pay them according to their performance and value, and if others hear about it, don't worry. It may incentivize them to work harder. Paying everyone an equal amount may not be exactly fair to those carrying the bigger load.

In the end, it's your company, but being understanding and fair, keeping harmony among your investigators, and making the tough decisions on who to keep employed is the way to go. Also, provide your investigators with the best equipment in order to get the job done right. Good equipment makes the job easier, fun, and increases success. Finally, realize that your investigators will likely work for other PIs as well; don't let this bother you. It may not be a sign of disloyalty, only a matter of making ends meet. It's difficult to sit around and maintain your financial needs while waiting for an assignment during a dry season. Investigators need to make a living, and by being available to other companies, they can do just that. Besides, the more they go out the better they become, and you reap the benefits.

10

Conclusion

FROM THE BEGINNING, my intention in writing this book was to give the reader a basic understanding of what it's like to do surveillance in the private sector, which is different from surveillance done in law enforcement and other government agencies. I tried framing it in a way that touched on many of the key aspects that could assist prospective private investigators in deciding if this work is something they can envision themselves doing, and if so, how to do it effectively.

I've also sent a humble message to fellow law-enforcement officers who are thinking of getting into this business and feel, as I once did, that private investigations should be a piece of cake. As a private investigator, I have been honored with the responsibility of introducing many individuals who have retired from law enforcement into the business of surveillance. Most, if not all, have quickly become aware of the immediate challenges in the private sector compared to their law-enforcement experience. And as a result, not many of them have remained. They may have gone to other areas in the private-investigative field where they felt more comfortable, and that's perfectly fine.

Surveillance is difficult, intense, exciting, and boring—all at the same time. I understand that it's not for everyone. Nevertheless, I've attempted in this book to encourage everyone interested in this field to give it a shot. As hard as it is, how will you know if you have what it takes if you don't try it? That's why I've mentioned that it really doesn't matter if you have law-enforcement experience or not or whether you're male or female. Even age may not matter to a certain extent.

I also must admit that although this business is hard, some have an advantage over others because of certain intangibles—things that cannot be taught, like instincts and a reliance on what your gut tells you. In some cases, you are simply born with this or have acquired it through your life experiences. I've observed a skill that fits into this category that I refer to as "vision."

Vision, as I describe it, is the ability to see things most people cannot easily see or detect. It's not necessarily a supernatural thing; it's just a more heightened perception. People who have this are able to identify a subject immediately, sometimes with just a partial view of the person. Or they're able to detect odd behaviors or changes in an environment. Identifying a subject from a photo, as mentioned earlier, is one of the most difficult challenges you will face. If you possess this skill, you've just set yourself apart from the pack and are extremely valuable to any company.

Now, if you don't have any of these unique abilities, you may still have a lot to offer. You may be good at planning, strategizing, researching the case file, or documenting details. You may be a dependable and dedicated hard worker. To use another sports term, "The best ability is availability." Being willing to work hard, learn, and think outside the box in order to achieve a desired outcome are also skills, as is an admirable work ethic. Hard work will not and should not go unnoticed and will provide you with even better opportunities down the road. The list of highly effective surveillance investigators is not long, so with a good effort, you should be able to jump to the top of the line quickly.

I've covered a lot of ground in this book but was not able to cover every single detail because there are so many variables and scenarios with each surveillance. Every surveillance has an identity of its own, and you need to treat each one like that. The moment you become complacent and begin to assume which operation is going to be easy and which one is going to be hard, you've already positioned yourself to fail. Just arrive at your assignments prepared for anything and make no assumptions or dinner plans.

Many of the things I've discussed in this book concerning strategies or tactics have been self-taught. I've done much reading and research to improve on my craft and discovered that others are also doing some of the things I'm doing. By the same token, I've also discovered that I have some interesting ideas and methods that others do not have. That's what inspired me to write this book. I do not consider myself to be the best or sole authority on surveillance. There are other people out there with unique ideas, perspectives, and skills on how to properly conduct a surveillance. The one thing I can say about myself is that when I go to work, my employer and the client get more than what they've paid for. In other words, I work hard. Whether they like the results or not, they've gotten an honest day's work from me.

I don't take an individual case personally, but what I do take personally is my performance and whether I've acted with integrity. In this line of work, you're out there alone without any supervision, and you can basically do and report whatever you want. But just remember that what you do in private when no one is watching is who you really are, and dishonesty has a way of exposing you. A lot of trust is being placed in you. Honor your employer and yourself with a good and honest effort every time you go out into the field. And I trust and believe that in some way, those efforts will be rewarded.

GLOSSARY

buffer cars: Vehicles that offer concealment between the investigator and the subject during a mobile surveillance.

burn: When the investigator, place, or thing has been compromised or made suspicious enough so that it is no longer viable.

canvass: A search conducted for the purpose of locating a person or thing.

date/time stamp: A feature on recording devices that displays the day and time of the recording.

mobile surveillance: Surveillance in a vehicle.

operator: Another term used for investigator.

quiet: Limiting your activity or movements in order to remain unnoticed.

spot-checking: Periodically checking in on the location of your subject by foot or vehicle because setting up an observation post within sight of the target location is not advisable.

subject: The person being followed or investigated.

target: Another term used for subject or a place or thing.

time shot: Periodic recordings randomly taken in order to provide proof that the investigator is where he or she is supposed to be.

www.ingramcontent.com/pod-product-compliance
Lightning Source LLC
Chambersburg PA
CBHW051811170526
45167CB00005B/1976